1 MONTH OF
FREE
READING

at

www.ForgottenBooks.com

By purchasing this book you are eligible for one month membership to ForgottenBooks.com, giving you unlimited access to our entire collection of over 700,000 titles via our web site and mobile apps.

To claim your free month visit:

www.forgottenbooks.com/free273233

ISBN 978-0-483-19323-9
PIBN 10273233

For support please visit www.forgottenbooks.com

SOME OF THE INFLUENCES AFFECTING MILK PRODUCTION

BY

LEROY ANDERSON

SOME OF THE INFLUENCES AFFECTING MILK PRODUCTION

WITH SPECIAL REFERENCE TO THE RELATION OF FOOD TO MILK FAT

———————

THESIS

PRESENTED TO THE

UNIVERSITY FACULTY OF CORNELL UNIVERSITY

FOR THE DEGREE OF

DOCTOR OF PHILOSOPHY

BY

LEROY ANDERSON, B. S., M. S. A.

———————

ITHACA, NEW YORK
JUNE, 1902

TABLE OF CONTENTS

INTRODUCTION

This paper contains a summary of investigations concerning the relation of food to milk-fat and the record of considerable original experimentation to determine the influence of food and of certain conditions of the cow upon the secretion of milk. That portion of the thesis which treats of the influence of food was prepared primarily for publication as Bulletin No. 173 of the Cornell University Agricultural Experiment Station. The experimental data obtained by Messrs. Johnson and Lauman from their experiments of 1896 and 1897 respectively were entirely worked over by the writer for publication in the above named bulletin, and is, therefore, considered to justly have a place in a paper of this kind. The report of the investigations concerning the relation of the temperature of the cow to the secretion of milk is offered as a line of study which is new in the field of animal production. The other chapters and the general summary contain some of the conclusions that are believed to be warranted by the knowledge concerning milk secretion which has been secured up to the present time by historical record and experimental research.

Acknowledgment is due Professor Henry H. Wing for his helpful suggestions during the progress of these investigations.

LEROY ANDERSON.

Cornell University,
    Ithaca, N. Y., June, 1902.

THE DEVELOPING INFLUENCES OF NATURAL ENVIRONMENT

The varied influences which go to make up the life of an individual or mould the character of an entire race are so many and so potent that it would be difficult to give to any one influence the place of first importance. Moreover, influences do not work singly in their effect upon organic life and it is, therefore, impossible to define the limits of each. It is more to the point and more satisfactory to discuss the leading factors which have had to do with organic development in a broad way, when we may the more clearly perceive the relation to each other of the minor forces which go to make up the main influences.

Among the strongest of these leading factors is the natural environment in which a breed or race of animals has been developed, *i. e.* the climate, soil, food and all of the other subtle forces which go to make up the habitat of an animal. It is not essential that the mind of man should have been present to guide the mating and care of individuals according to some preconceived and fixed type. Differences in the determining natural forces named above, in which man plays only as an added force in the natural selection, are sufficient to develop races of animals possessing characters so widely varying as to form what we call breeds. That the different breeds of cattle sprang from one source is believed to be one of the established facts in the evolution of animal life. "The systematic naturalist, who generally knows nothing of the art of breeding, who does not pretend to know how and when the several domestic races were formed, who cannot have seen the intermediate gradations, for they do not now exist, nevertheless feels no doubt that these races are sprung from a single source."*

We have but to notice the changes made in animal form, or in the production of meat and milk during the past half century, to make it readily conceivable that the antipodes of breed characteristics could have developed from one parent stock during the

---

* Darwin. Animals and Plants under Domestication, Vol. II, p. 233.

ages which cattle have undoubtedly been upon the earth. The most noted and remarkable differences are found between the cattle whose whole tendency is to produce meat and those whose tendency is to produce milk. But it is more to our point to consider the latter only and amongst these varieties are found breeds which show marked characteristics. No better illustration of opposites in development in dairy cattle could be imagined than is afforded by the Jersey cattle on the one hand and the Holstein-Friesian on the other. Their differences are indicated in form, size, and quantity and quality of milk.

The history of Holstein-Friesian cattle is known, in legend at least, for more than two thousand years, and the important part in their history is a study of the soil, climate and food which made up the formative portion of their environment during this long period. The native home of these cattle is that portion of The Netherlands lying contiguous to the North Sea where the climate is cool and moist, both by reason of much fog and a high degree of precipitation. The soil is of that dense, clayey nature which, with the large amount of moisture prevailing induces a luxuriant growth of grass. This combination also produces a pasturage which carries a high percentage of water and a correspondingly low content of dry or nutrient substance.

Holland dairy practice has been, for the most part, to have the cows calve during the spring months so as to have them in the flush of milking when turned from winter stable to pasture. The cows, then, during their heaviest milking period and during the time when they were obliged to consume the most food in order to produce milk as well as to maintain life and growth, were forced to obtain the needed sustenance from the prevailing luxuriant but watery grass. In order to secure sufficient nourishment, the cow must take into her body large amounts of this succulent food, and the natural result of such feeding was to develop a large abdomen with a correspondingly large digestive capacity. The correlative effect upon the size was to make it larger and upon the bony structure to make it somewhat coarse and angular. But what is more to our present purpose is the effect of these large quantities of watery food upon milk production. The natural result has been to induce a flow of milk which is not equaled in quantity by any other breed of cattle and which carries a lower percentage of butter fat and other solids than the milk of any other of the improved dairy breeds.

Quite opposite to the above conditions were those under which the Jersey cattle have been developed. Their native Isle in the English Channel possesses a climate made mild and equable by the Gulf Stream, and one much dryer than the climate of North Holland and Friesland. The soil is a light loam, carrying in connection with the relatively light precipitation, an herbage which is not abundant, but is comparatively high in nutritive substance and low in water content. Whether the Jersey cow were at pasture or whether stall fed, at no time was she obliged to consume large quantities of succulent food in order to provide the nourishment that her system required. Her digestive organs were not, therefore, unduly distended and the correlative effect of her food conditions were such as to develop a moderately sized body and a rather fine bony structure. In the production of milk, the result of her environment and food has been to produce a moderate amount which is richer in fat and other solids than the milk of any other breed of cattle.

That the wide variations found between the breeds under discussion are due in a large degree to different conditions of soil, climate and food is believed to be quite true. What the original type of animal was in either case before coming under the influences where history records their beginning as distinct breeds, no one knows. What they are to-day and what has been their habitat for centuries is known to all readers of animal history. There can be but one conclusion, viz., that the natural conditions and exigencies which go to make up the environment of the respective countries are responsible in the largest degree for the dissimilarity between the two breeds.

To-day the Jersey and Holstein-Friesian cattle are battling for dairy supremacy in the same field. They have been in this country in large numbers for a quarter of a century, and the change in environment is being watched with deep interest. Here they have been subjected to similar conditions of food, care and climate. On the one hand, the Jerseys have experienced a change to a more succulent ration in the shape of corn

silage and like forage crops than their native Isle afforded. On the other, the Holstein-Friesians have been fed more concentrated food and been obliged to range more over scant and hilly pastures than they were accustomed to do at home. If there be any definite change it is difficult to prove it by experimental data. Breeders of Jerseys claim that the American type is larger and coârser than the Island progenitor and also than the Island type of to-day. It is also claimed that they yield a greater amount of milk and of no decreasing quality. Leading breeders of Holstein-Friesians claim that the American type is finer in form and bony structure, and gives richer milk than the Holland ancestors. They contend also that the quantity of milk has not decreased while the quality has been improving. None of these claims as to milking qualities can be substantiated by accurate data because no records of milk production were kept twenty-five years ago as to-day. There is, however, no reason for doubting the claims, for if we question them we would also question the possibility of the improvement of animals, of which there can be no doubt. That the larger and coarser animal should grow smaller and finer and the smaller and finer animal grow larger and coarser, when changed from the natural habitat which had produced that largeness or smallness, to one and the same land and to like conditions, is of interest and value in bearing out the conclusions as to the influence of natural environment in moulding the form and characteristics of animals to so great an extent as to build up different breeds.

Another set of influences which is of very great moment in the development of individuals and of races is that due to heredity. Without this factor any effect which environment may have upon one generation would be of no value to the succeeding generation. It is not to the purpose here to discuss heredity in all of its ramifications, but rather to point to the larger phases of the subject which have been found to be most instrumental in the upbuilding of the animal kingdom and especially the dairy cow as it is found to-day. It will be sufficient at the outset to take for a theme, the possibility that any or all characteristics may be transmitted from generation to generation and that whatever affects the parent may find expression also in the offspring.

We have seen that the Holstein-Friesian cattle have, through many centuries, developed a capacity for producing large amounts of milk. We have seen that the Jersey cattle have, through possibly a less number of centuries, developed a capacity for producing a milk very rich in total solid substance. Did we carry the study further we would find the Herefords following a development that has induced the formation of flesh and not of milk except to a very small degree. Still further we would find the Shorthorns represented on the one hand by a portion of the breed resembling the Hereford in meat and non-milk producing power, and on the other hand by another portion of the breed resembling somewhat the milking characteristics of the Holland cattle and also the flesh producing feature of a more approved beef strain.

These varied and quite opposite characteristics are due in the first place to those conditions which have been discussed in the preceding chapter. A change in the food or habit of the animal induces a change in the organic being in order to render the animal at home in its environment. In other words a variation from the parental type has occurred, which variation will be permanent within the individual depending upon the permanency of the altered environment. This variation may be good or bad according to the character of the outward influence. If the change be in the direction of more and better food, more comfortable quarters and more hygienic use the resultant variation is quite sure to be a beneficent one, and vice versa.

The possibility of variation entering the life and function of an individual is dependent upon the fundamental principle of the mutability of all organic beings, which in turn finds its origin in the mobile nature of the living plasm of the cells that combine to make up the organic being. Changes in form of any portion of the animal body are due to a change in the nutrition and use of that portion. The function of an organ is not readily altered, but its capacity for production or secretion may be easily influenced, e. g., the function of the epithelial cells of the udder is to secrete milk; abundance or scarcity of food, good or bad use, may alter the amount of milk produced, but nothing can change the primal function of the organ. Upon the fixedness of function may be based the certainty of the inheritance of organic life and upon the mobility of cellular protoplasm, the principle of variation without which there could be no improvement.

Given a permanent variation in an individual its offspring are born with a tendency in a like direction, which tendency may be accentuated by a continuance of the conditions causing the parental variation. Improvement in animals begun by a desirable variation is, then, carried toward perpetuation by selecting for breeding those individuals which show the most advancement under the bettered environment. Improvement is most rapid when the mind of man is present to guide the selection in the direction of a preconceived standard. But even if a preconceived ideal be not before the breeder's eye, he will unconsciously mate such animals as show the most variation in the desired direction, i. e., those which conform most readily to the environment in which he has placed them.

The power of selection in rendering aid in animal improvement depends upon the presence of variability, for were there no variability between animals there would be no need for the practice of selection. Selection in breeding has been the most powerful ally of environment in moulding breed characteristics. In fact, so far as man's work is concerned it may be said to be

the chief controlling force. By means of selection in taking advantage of the effects of environment, the world now possesses its highly developed breeds of domestic animals. It may overcome even the natural tendencies of food in developing a breed. The possibility is that the native foods of the Tees valley and of North Holland are such as to tend to build a race of cattle to produce meat and milk respectively. But had the men who are responsible for the breeds which there originated, selected those Shorthorns which showed the greatest tendencies toward milk production and the Holstein-Friesians showing the strongest leanings toward meat production, the probability is that the present classification in which these two breeds find themselves would be reversed. We have previously referred to such a possibility in the fact that part of the Shorthorn breed is looked upon as dairy stock. The difference between them and their beef producing sisters was brought about wholly by a system of selection.

In the light of these facts we may even say that man is able to direct the course of food nutrients in the animal by his use of the power of selection. If he wishes to change a beef producing breed to a milk standard his plan is to breed from such individuals as show the strongest dairy tendency, although that tendency be at first slight. In other words the breeder is transferring the disposition of the animal's food from building tissue or body fat to the work of secreting milk in the udder. There is not necessarily any change in the process of digestion ; there is no change in function of individual organs; the change is in the degree or extent of the function by lessening the activity of flesh producing cells and increasing that of the cells which secrete milk. By reversing the method of selection a dairy breed may be changed to one producing beef.

The influence of selection in thus transforming cattle is greatly enhanced by man's care of the milk secreting organ. By irregular and incomplete milking, the secretion tends to decline in quantity until it ceases altogether, when if the same food supply be continued, the animal lays on flesh. On the other hand, regular, careful and complete withdrawal of milk from the udder tends to keep up the milk flow. It is upon this basis that the domesticated cow has been developed into a state of giving milk for a year or more continuously, when in her wild, native condition, the period of lactation was only of sufficient length to provide food for the calf until he was old and strong enough to subsist upon other food. An approximation to the wild state is found to-day among the cattle upon the large stock ranges. Often one of the cows is taken from the range herd with the view of making a milch cow of her, but there is always disappointment, for her milk flows only for a few months at the most. Her environment and the method of selection has been such that she inherits a tendency for a brief period of lactation. By proper food and use and wise selection this tendency may be gradually overcome until her descendants, several generations removed, will possess a lactation period of approved duration.

Phenomena such as here described may not be substantiated by what are to-day considered authentic experimental data. Nevertheless they are a matter of history which is held to be true by all reliable testimony. The influences of heredity as here outlined are slow in working out these changes in production, which to the uninformed may appear beyond the realm of possibility.

Referring to the immediate influence of heredity upon the secretion of milk we find experimental data largely wanting, both in extent and in the certainty of conclusions. One example will serve to illustrate : Cederholm * furnishes some data upon the influence of heredity on the quality of cows' milk and says that three of the bulls used caused a marked improvement in the quality of the milk produced by their offspring. One bull had five daughters, each of which gave poorer milk than her dam. This bull was out of a cow that produced milk having an average per cent of fat of 3.06. "In general the greatest improvement was observed in case of cows producing the poorest grades of milk. The data so far secured on this point are not considered sufficient to permit of definite conclusions as to the relative influence of the ancestors of a cow on the quality of milk produced by her, but they show, at any rate, that the bull exerts a a decided influence for better or worse on the milk product of his progeny. "

---

* Landmannen, 11 (1900) p. 57, Abs. E. S. R. by F. W. Woll.

Tabulations of records in a similar way have been made in other instances by various parties, but the usual result is that the data are insufficient to furnish conclusive evidence. The fact is that systematic records of milk production, and especially of the quality of the milk, are of so recent beginning in dairy practice that it is extremely difficult to secure a line of descent of sufficient length to furnish data possessing experimental value. The influences which have developed the present milking powers of the dairy breeds have been working for centuries and every evidence adds to the belief that heredity works slowly in improving the quantity or quality of any animal product. No short cut has yet been discovered whereby the individual yield of milk or butter may be doubled among the members of the improved breeds. On the other hand no one who is conversant with the history of cattle will admit that there is not yet room for large improvement. But the increase in production must come through a careful fostering of such environmental conditions as will induce desirable variations and then seeking to perpetuate those variations through methodical selection.

THE INFLUENCE OF FOOD

There are two main divisions of the question concerning the relation of food to milk secretion. On the one hand is the relation of food supply to the quantity of milk produced and on the other its relation to the quality of the milk by which is usually meant the proportion of butter fat present. So far as the quantity is concerned there is no doubt as to the immediate and ultimate effect of the food supply. Given an abundant supply of food furnishing nourishment in all necessary nutrients and we may expect as large a flow of milk as the capacity of the cow will permit. Let the food supply be restricted either in total digestible substance or in the essential nutrients and the yield of milk will be less than the normal capacity of the cow. All experiments bearing upon this subject have shown the intimate relation between food supply and the yield of milk.

Concerning the relation of food to milk-fat, experimental research has been somewhat contradictory. Some experiments have seemed to indicate that certain foods possess the power of increasing the proportion of fat in milk, while others, and much the larger number, show that the variations in the quality of milk are not traceable to the food. All who are familiar with the handling of milk know that variations in the per cent of fat do exist and this with the same cow on the same feed and under uniform environment. Why the quality of milk fluctuates so widely under conditions which to all outward appearances are the same, has never been determined experimentally.

Experiments conducted for the purpose of determining the relation of food to milk production have usually shown that where a sudden and radical change in the food has taken place, this change has been accompanied by a more than ordinary variation in the per cent of fat. This variation may be either an increase or a decrease. After the cows become accustomed to the new feed their milk returns to its former average per cent of fat, which may be called the normal per cent. Such phenomena would seem to indicate that the per cent of fat in milk is subject to the peculiar constitution of the cow and that she will give milk of a certain average composition so long as nothing occurs to disturb the " even tenor of her way."

A definite knowledge of the relation of food to milk-fat would solve the question as to whether or not the per cent of fat may be permanently increased by feeding. But concerning this point we have little information except theories based upon the results of many experiments. One theory has been long and largely held that milk-fat is produced from the protein in the food. If this were the case a natural supposition would be that by increasing the amount of protein in the food, the proportion of fat in the milk would be thereby increased. Another theory is that milk-fat is produced from the fat in the food. Then feeding an increased amount of fat might be supposed to result in a higher per cent of fat in the milk; or, on the other hand, a decrease in the supply of food-fat would likewise cause a decrease in the per cent of milk-fat. A third theory, and the one which is most largely entertained, is that so long as the animal is well nourished the per cent of fat in the milk is not appreciably affected by even wide variations in the character of the food. Experiments supporting these three theories will be found in subsequent pages.

The question has a practical bearing in the economical management of the dairy. For, if by food we may increase the richness of the milk, then there is opportunity to enhance the value of all our cows. Butter-fat is the most valuable constituent of milk, and if the cow may be made to produce a milk richer in fat by giving her certain foods, or foods containing a large proportion of a particular nutrient, then the dairyman may increase the value of his cows to the extent that they may be made to respond to the particular foods by increased production of fat. Again if feeding large amounts of protein tend to an increased production of milk-fat, then the dairyman will need to purchase foods containing a high proportion of protein, which foods usually command higher prices than those containing less protein. If, on the other hand, a large supply of protein is not essential to the production of milk-fat; or, if it is not governed by the food so long as the cow is well nourished, then the dairyman is warranted in feeding those cheaper foods which contain less protein and more carbohydrates and fat.

The experimental work which has come within the immediate

notice or supervision of the writer upon this mooted question is herein described. The record is given of two long experiments with rations having different nutritive ratios, and also a less extended one with a ration containing varying quantities of palm nut meal. Considerable space is given to a summary of the leading experiments relating to the influence of food on milk production with especial reference to the quality of the milk, by which is meant here its percentage of fat. The records of these experiments are gleaned from all reliable sources both domestic and foreign. In collecting this data free use has been made of all experimental literature obtainable and reference is usually made to the original article. The Experiment Station Record has been used freely, especially for translations of foreign experiments which are reported in periodicals not found in the University library. The attempt has been to make this summary as brief as possible and yet give a fair idea of the plan and scope of the experiment, together with the results or conclusions obtained.

SUMMARY OF EXPERIMENTS CONCERNING THE RELATION OF FOOD TO MILK-FAT

Jordan[*] experimented on five cows with three different kinds of rations during three periods, the rations being made up so as to contain varying amounts of vegetable fats, and found that the yield of milk diminished somewhat in passing from the ration rich in fat to the one containing less fat, and increased slightly after changing again to the fat rich ration. "The composition of the milk varied but little and no more, or even less, during the three periods than is often observed when the ration is not changed."

In a later experiment [†] Jordan fed three cows during three periods of 35 days each on two rations, one having a nutritive ratio of 1:6.7 and the other 1:12.3 and found that "the yield of milk from the nitrogenous ration was from one-fifth to more than one-third larger than that from the carbonaceous ration. In general the milk was materially richer while the cows were

---

* Maine Station Annual Report, 1891, p. 62.
† Same 1893, p. 73.

fed the ration rich in protein. * * * The composition of the milk solids seemed to be independent of the ration. In general the proportion of fat increased throughout the experiment without regard to what the cows were fed, and no evidence is furnished in support of the notion that by changing the food it is possible to produce more butter-fat without an accompanying increased production of the other milk solids."

Whitcher,* after studying the effect of pasture and silage, and of changing the nutritive ratio on the quality of the milk, found very little variation in the per cent of fat and concludes: "I feel warranted in saying that a given animal by heredity is so constituted that she will give a milk of certain average composition; by judicious or injudicious feeding the amount of milk may be largely varied, but the quality of the product will be chiefly determined by the individuality of the cow."

Wood,† in experimenting on the effect of some coarse fodders on quantity and quality of milk during several experimental periods of two weeks each, found "no variation in the quality of the milk that could be attributed to the character of the food."

Later,‡ he fed three cows for two weeks on a basal ration of silage, clover hay, vetch hay, oats and middlings. Then in three subsequent periods of two weeks each, palm oil, cottonseed oil, corn oil, oleo oil, cocoanut oil and stearin were fed to different cows at the rate of 12 ounces per 1,000 pounds live weight, making a nutritive ratio of 1:6.8. The conclusions reached were: "That the first effect of an increase of fat in a cow's ration is to increase the per cent of fat in her milk."

"That with the continuance of such a ration the tendency is for the milk to return to its normal condition."

"That the increase in fat is not due to the oils but to the unnatural character of the ration."

"That the results of this experiment tend to confirm the conclusions expressed in previous bulletins from this Station; that the composition of a cow's milk is determined by the individuality of the cow, and that although an unusual food may dis-

---

*New Hampshire Station Bulletin 9, 1890.
† Same, Bulletin 18, 1892.
‡ Same, Bulletin 20, 1894.

turb for a time the composition of the milk, its effect is not continuous.''

Hills* studied the effect of heavy feeding of grains on milk production by giving two cows for two months a continually increasing amount of grain until they were receiving all they would eat.   He found that there was little change in the composition of the milk on increasingly heavy grain feeding, and that no connection could be traced between the quality of the milk and the food given.

Hills†, in a series of feeding tests covering five periods of four weeks each, and using thirty-one cows, experimented with various coarse fodders, grains and mixed feeds.   The invariable conclusion was that there was no material change in the quality of the milk as a result of the change in ration.

Hills ‡ reports that unemulsified cottonseed oil and emulsified cottonseed, corn and linseed oils were fed with bran or corn meal and bran, hay and silage, as against the same rations without the oil.   Milk yields to the unit of dry matter eaten were always increased when oil was fed, the increase amounting from three to nine per cent.   The amount of total solids and fat was increased by the cottonseed oil feeding from two to fifteen per cent, on linseed oil feeding two per cent and on corn oil feeding not at all.   The quality of milk was always improved at the outset of this class of feeding but quickly returned to normal quality or became poorer than usual when corn or linseed oils were fed.   The increased fat percentage—unaccompanied by rise in the percentage of solids not fat—was fairly permanent, lasting from four to six weeks, when either raw or emulsified cottonseed oil was fed.   The length of feeding periods was four to five weeks.

Hills ‖ conducted a series of experiments to learn the effect of adding an excessive amount of single nutrients to a cow's ration. The feeding periods were four weeks long, of which the first ten days were considered preliminary.   His general summary is:

---

* Vermont Station, Annual Report, 1890, p. 75.

† Same, 1895, p. 203.

‡ Same, 1899, p. 269.

‖ Same, 1900, p. 417.

"The addition of about one-fifth more digestible protein (in Atlantic gluten flour) to a ration of amounts of this nutrient greater than standard requirements was practically without effect as a milk stimulant. The addition of about one-fifth more digestible carbohydrates (in brown sugar) to a ration containing amounts of these nutrients equal to or in excess of standard requirements had little or no effect upon either the quantity or quality of the milk. The addition of a solid fat (palm oil) to a ration already containing digestible ether extract in excess of standard requirements increased its digestible fat content about one-half. It had a slight effect upon the quantity and a pronounced effect upon the quality of the milk. The total solid percentage was increased two per cent (0.24 per -cent) and the fat seven per cent. (0.36 per cent). The increase seems to have been a permanent one.

Cooke, * in reporting an experiment in feeding sugar meal, cream gluten meal and germ meal to nine cows for four months in periods of four weeks each, says: "We are led to the conclusion that sugar meal and cream gluten have a slight effect toward an increase in the richness of the milk."

Lindsey† fed six cows in nine and fourteen-day periods with seven days preliminary feeding to each period on rations containing amounts of protein which varied from 1.3 to 3.76 pounds per head daily, and the nutritive ratio varied from 1:4.4 to 1:10. The periods were rather short, but the "indications are that the composition of the milk, especially the fat, appeared to be favorably affected by the addition of protein up to three pounds, although there was considerable difference in the cows in this respect."

Lindsey, Holland and Billings‡ varied the nutritive ratio of the ration from 1:3.86 to 1:9.43 while feeding six cows in two lots of three each, during four periods of 21 to 26 days each, with a seven-day preliminary period. They conclude: "That the same amount of digestible matter in the narrow rations produced from 11.8 to 12.9 per cent more milk than did a like amount of

---

* Vermont Station, Bulletin 31, 1892.
† Massachusetts (State) Station Annual Report, 1894, p. 42.
‡ Massachusetts (Hatch) Station, Annual Report. 1896, p. 100.

digestible matter in the wide rations, and that neither the narrow nor wide rations produced any decided change in the composition of the milk."

Lindsey* summarizes the results of a series of experiments extending over a period of six years in which was studied the effect upon milk production of feeding rations containing varying amounts of protein and of oil (in flaxseed meal). He concludes that "Different amounts of protein do not seem to have any influence on the composition of the milk. Linseed oil in flaxseed meal, when fed in considerable quantities (1.40 pounds of digestible oil daily), increased the fat percentage and decreased the nitrogenous matter of the milk. This fat increase was only temporary, the milk gradually returning (in four or five weeks) to its normal fat content. The nitrogenous matter also gradually returned to normal, but more slowly than the fat. In general, feeds containing much oil have a tendency to slightly increase the fat content of milk when first fed. The fat percentage gradually returns to normal."

Jordan and Jentner‡ changed the ration of a cow in three ways : "(1) By decreasing the fat in the food from about the usual quantity to practically none; (2) by producing wide variations in the protein supply and nutritive ratio, and (3) by producing wide variations in the supply of total digestible material." The cow was "fed ninety-five days on a ration from which the fats had been nearly all extracted, and she continued to secrete milk similar to that produced when fed on the same kinds of hay and grain in their normal condition." The food-fat eaten during this time was 11.6 pounds, 5.7 pounds of which was digested, while the yield of milk-fat was 62.9 pounds. Throughout the whole experiment, "the composition of the milk bore no definite relation to the amount and kind of food."

Jordan, Jentner and Fuller ‡ later conducted similar experiments in which three cows were used : "Cow 12 fed a fat-poor ration in which the protein supply was gradually decreased from 2.6 pounds daily to 1.6 pounds and then gradually restored to

---

* Massachusetts (Hatch) Station, Annual Report, 1900, p. 14.
† New York (State) Station, Bulletin 132, 1897.
‡ Same, Bulletin 197, 1901.

the maximum, with accompanying increase and decrease in carbohydrates so that the digestible dry matter of the ration was
kept fairly uniform ; Cow 10 fed a ration with normal supply of
fat at first which was gradually increased to 1.4 pounds daily, then
gradually restored to the normal; Cow 2 fed the herd ration having
a nutritive ratio about 1.5.6. These rations were quite varied in
character and contained some fat-extracted foods ; yet showed a
quite uniform digestibility of about 70 per cent of the dry matter. It is believed that this figure represents fairly the digestibility of rations made up in part of silage and containing a fair
proportion of high class grains. A widening of the nutritive
ratios appeared to render rations less digestible, especially the
protein. The marked changes in protein content and in fat content of rations did not produce noticeable changes in the character or composition of the milk. In the former test, during 59
days, 18.4 pounds of fat was formed in the milk which could
not have had its source in food-fat or food-protein and could
hardly have been drawn from the cow's body fat as she increased
in weight 33 pounds in the same time. In this test Cow 12 in
74 days produced 39 pounds of fat similarly unaccounted for,
with a body gain of 15 pounds ; and Cow 2, in 4 days 1¼ pounds.
These amounts of fat must have come from the carbohydrates in
the food.''

''A lessening of protein supply in the food did not produce a
corresponding decrease of protein in the milk solids, but caused
a marked lessening of protein decomposition in the body. * *

'' Over 40 per cent of the available energy value of the rations
was used for maintenance, over 30 per cent reappeared in the
milk solids, leaving a balance of from one-fifth to one-fourth of
the ration. The logical conclusion is that this balance, in part
at least, sustains the work of milk secretion.''

Wing * added ordinary beef tallow to the usual grain ration
of ten cows, giving them at first four ounces per head, and
increasing the amount gradually until each cow was consuming
two pounds daily, which amount was fed for six or seven weeks.
He found '' no increase in the per cent of fat in the milk as a
result of feeding tallow in addition to a liberal grain ration.''

---

* New York (Cornell) Station, Bulletin 92, 1895.

Waters and Hess * gave rations varying in nutritive ratio from 1:3.9 to 1:6.65 to nine cows through four periods of thirty days each, and say : "It appears that the narrower nutritive ratio tended to increase the per cent of fat."

Farrington † studied the effect of heavy grain feeding by giving three cows from Dec. 1 to June 1, in eight periods ranging from 6 to 51 days, an amount of grain increasing continually from 12 to 24 pounds per head daily where it was held for two months, when it was decreased gradually until the cows went to pasture, May 1. The nutritive ratio varied from 1:4 to 1:9.4. He found " that the increase of feed was accompanied by a considerable increase in the pounds of milk produced, and consequently in the pounds' of solids, fat, and solids not fat in the milk ; but with the exception of one or two days, there were no greater changes in the percentages of fat in the milk after the increase of feed than before it was made."

Wilson, Kent, Curtiss and Patrick ‡ compared corn and cob meal with sugar meal by feeding them to four cows in alternating periods of 21 days each with a 10-day preliminary period, and conclude that "quality of milk, so far as measured by its percentage of fat, was changed by feed to a much greater degree than was quantity. Sugar meal produced 17 per cent more fat and six per cent more total solids per 100 pounds of milk than did the corn and cob meal."

Armsby, ‖ during three periods of three weeks each with two cows compared bran with corn meal and found that while there were slight changes in the composition of the milk there was " no indication that the feeding had anything to do with these changes." Again in comparing in a similar manner bran with oil meal there were slight changes as before, but " we may safely conclude that whatever changes took place in the composition of the milk-solids were due to advancing lactation and not to the feed."

* Pennsylvania Station, Annual Report, 1895, p. 56.
† Illinois Station, Bulletin 24, 1894.
‡ Iowa Station Bulletin 14, 1891.
‖ Wisconsin Station Annual Report 1886, pp. 115 and 130.

Woll,[*] in comparing the feeding value of ground oats and bran for milk production, found that "the cows invariably did better on oats, going up in milk yield when coming on oats and going down when bran was fed, while the fat content of the milk remained the same on an average."

Linfield [†] studied the effect of two rations varying in nutritive ratio on the per cent of fat in milk with ten cows during eight periods of three weeks each. He concludes, "this test adds but another item to the fairly well established fact that an increase in the quantity of concentrated food in the ration of a cow, does not increase the richness of the milk provided the cows are well fed to start with."

Dean [‡] carried on experiments during several years to ascertain the effect of food on the quality and quantity of milk. The results obtained from feeding coarse fodder with and without grain, from comparing pasturage with and without grain, from feeding slop, and from other experiments, generally agree with this statement made in Bulletin No. 80, that "the general conclusion would seem to be that the food does not effect the quality of the milk to any appreciable extent so long as the animals are in good condition."

Speir [||] reports as least three different experiments on the effect of foods on milk production. He tested a large number of different kinds of feeding stuffs both singly and in various combinations during periods of four to five weeks in length. Some of his conclusions are that "an increase of oil in the food does not seem to give any increase of fat in the milk. Rations having an extremely high albuminoid ratio seem to have a depressing effect on the milk yield, well mixed foods giving the best results in this respect. Every food when first given, seems to have more or less effect in increasing or decreasing the percentage of fat in the milk. This effect, however, is transitory and the milk returns to its normal composition about the end of the first week."

---

[*] Wisconsin Station Annual Report 1890, p. 65.

[†] Utah Station, Bulletin 43, 1895.

[‡] Ontario Agricultural College and Farm Report 1891, p. 154; 1893, p. 148; 1894, pp. 147 and 148.

[||] Transactions of the Highland and Agricultural Society, Scotland, 1894, p. 83; 1896, p. 269; 1897, p. 296.

Stohman,[*] in experimenting with goats found that the fat content of the milk was proportional to the fat content of the fodder, but that by a great increase in the nitrogenous foods, the milk-fat did not increase in the same way as when the fat content of the food was increased.

Kühn[†] carried on extensive feeding trials with bean meal, palm nut cake and malt sprouts, having in all 42 experiments with 10 cows. The feeding periods varied from 21 to 47 days in length. The grains were fed separately in addition to a normal ration and in quantities of 1.5, 2 and 3 kilograms per head daily. According to his results the fat content of the milk increased proportionately with the increase of protein fed, but did not decrease in the same proportion when the protein in the food was decreased. He concludes " that the palm nut cake exerted on the whole a favorable influence upon milk production and especially upon the fat content of the milk. " The bean meal and malt sprouts did not have a like favorable effect. He found that the addition of one-half kilogram of oil to the ration increased the quantity and quality of the milk. But he considered " that this added fat had no *direct* influence on milk production ; that it has an indirect effect in this manner : that a certain quantity of protein is thereby made available for milk production which before the feeding of the fat was used in sustaining the animal body, but the fat now performs this office and permits the protein to be used for producing milk. " He concludes also " that these experiments, according to all observations, prove in the clearest manner how greatly the milk production, and the possibility of influencing arbitrarily through feeding the amount or composition of the product, are dependent upon the individuality of the animal. "

Heinrich[‡] compared peanut cake with cocoanut cake, the latter ration containing 350 grams more fat than the former. The rations were alternated in periods of four weeks each and three cows were used. He found that the fat of the milk was considerably increased both in percentage and total amount, when the

[*] Journal für Landwirtschaft, 1868, pp. 135, 307 and 420.

[†] Same, 25, (1877), p. 332.

[‡] Abs. in Experiment Station Record 3 (1891), p. 67.

cocoanut ration was fed, but there was much difference in the animals regarding this point. It is his opinion that the increased yield of fat may be accounted for by the increased amount of fat in the food.

Kochs and Ramm *·fed three cows during four periods of about four weeks each, on rations which contained practically the same amounts of dry matter, and nearly equal amounts of digestible non-nitrogenous matter, but the amount of protein fed was such as to make the nutritive ratio vary from 1:8.19 to 1:5.42 to 1:4.31 and to 1:8.19 in the successive periods. They found that "the proportional fat content of the milk remained unchanged by the very wide changes in the food."

Klein † found that the addition of sunflower cake to the usual ration of four cows was followed by an increased milk yield, while it seemed to have no specific effect on the fat content of the milk.

Maercker and Morgen‡ report a series of coöperative experiments with farmers in which the effect of watery foods on milk secretion was studied. Beet diffusion residue (beet pulp) was fed alone and also with potato residue (from starch manufacture) in addition to a basal ration of hay, straw and grain. The amounts of residue fed daily were such as to give quantities of water ranging from 43 to 150 pounds per head. The experimental periods were ten days each. They found that the quantity of milk increased regularly with the increase of watery food up to 116 pounds, and that the increase in watery food was without discernible effect upon the composition of the milk.

Juretschke ‖ has found as a result of the addition of 4 to 5 pounds, per thousand pounds live weight, of cottonseed cake, rape cake, and peanut cake to a basal ration consisting of hay, straw, brewers' grains and wheat bran, that the "milk secretion is not directly but only indirectly affected by feeding and that the feeding of large amounts of fat does not increase the amount of butter-fat in the milk."

---

* Landwirtschaftliche Jahrbücher 21 (1892) p, 809.
† Milch Zeitung 21 (1892) p. 673.
‡ Abs. in Experiment Station Record, 3 (1892) p. 557.
‖ Molkerei Zeitung 7 (1893) p. 518.

Backhaus * found by feeding ten cows on a basal ration of hay, straw, brewers' grains, etc., and alternating in periods of two weeks with peanut cake, palm nut cake and cottonseed oil cake, that in order to bring about changes in the fat content of milk very little can be accomplished by the kind of food, and that the favorable effect of some concentrated foods which have been found to increase the fat takes place only when large quantities are fed.

Soxhlet † reports some investigations on the production of milk richer in fat. He says nothing of the plan or extent of his experiments and gives nothing but the conclusions and a discussion of theories. As compared with hay alone, the addition of fourteen pounds of starch, treated with malt and given as a sweet drink, with sixteen pounds of hay made no appreciable increase in milk yield but a noticeable decrease (about 0.7 per cent) in fat. The fat content was practically the same when four pounds of rice gluten containing 71 per cent of protein was fed as when hay was fed alone. When sesame oil, linseed oil or tallow was added to the ration in the form of emulsions thoroughly mixed with the drinking water, the milk contained as high as 5.8 per cent of fat. When 1.5 to 2 pounds of linseed oil were added to 18 to 22 pounds of hay the milk averaged 5.24 per cent of fat for four days ; when 1 to 2 pounds of tallow were added to the same amount of hay the milk contained from 4.24 to 5.5 per cent of fat, the average for eight days being 4.7 per cent. The author believes that the addition of oils to the ration in the form of emulsions will increase the per cent of fat in the milk while the addition of the same oils in other forms will not so increase it, because the oils are more easily digested in the form of emulsion. He does not believe that the fat of the food goes directly into the milk, but that it forces the body fat, i. e. tallow, over into the milk, and thus indirectly increases the quantity of milk-fat. He further states that the fat of the food alone, and not the protein or carbohydrates, is capable of bringing about a one-sided increase in the fat content of the milk.

---

* Journal für Landwirtschaft 41 (1893) p. 328.
† Abs. Experiment Station Record, 8 (1897), p. 1016.

Beglarian * studied the effect of linseed oil, given in water as an emulsion and of ground flaxseed with four cows during four periods of eight days each. The cows shrank in milk yield while taking the oil ration and increased on the flaxseed ration. The author considers the results entirely negative since the oil was not accompanied by an appreciable rise in the fat content, while it had an unfavorable effect on the digestion and comfort of the cows. The ground flaxseed had no effect on the quality of the milk and a less unfavorable influence on the animal's digestion.

Holtsmark † found that feeding cows as much as 77 pounds of turnips per head daily in connection with a liberal ration of concentrated feed and cut straw, caused no decrease in the fat content of the herd milk, as compared with the feeding of the regular ration of hay, straw, concentrated feed and a small quantity of roots.

Ramm,‡ to study the effect of different foods on milk production gave ten cows a basal ration consisting of 14 kg. of hay, 6 kg. straw and 50 kg. of beets, to which, for periods of ten days each, he added separately eighteen different foods. He found much variation in the fat content of the milk but no marked increase except with palm nut cake (7.91 kg.) alone and with a mixture of equal parts (8.25 kg.) of palm nut cake and beet molasses, this mixture being accompanied with a higher per cent of fat and total fat in the milk than any other food. For this reason the author thinks molasses has a greater effect on the quality of milk than palm nut cake. He found no relation between the fat content of the milk and the fat content of the food.

In a later experiment, Ramm made further comparison of the feeding value of various molasses mixtures. The mixtures used were peat molasses (80 per cent molasses and 20 per cent peat), liquid molasses, equal parts of molasses and palm nut meal, molasses pulp (molasses mixed with fresh potato pulp and dried), molasses chips (fresh beet pulp and molasses mixed and dried), barley meal and palm nut cake of average quality. The basal

---

* Milch Zeitung 26 (1897) p. 522.
† Abs. in Experiment Station Record, 9 (1897) p. 92, by F. W. Woll.
‡ Landwirtschaftliche Jahrbücher 26 (1897) pp. 693, 731.

ration consisted of hay, straw and beets. There were seven experimental periods of 20 days each, the last five days only being used in comparison. Eight cows were used. He found the barley meal to excel the molasses preparations for milk production, but concludes that the latter induce an increase in the fat content of the milk.

Winternitz* fed a goat on sesame oil mixed with a small amount of iodin. He found a portion of the iodin was absorbed by the milk-fat and thus concludes that a direct transmission of the fat of the food into the milk may take place.

Albert and Maercker† studied the effect of rations rich and poor in fat, on ten cows during six periods ranging from 7 to 18 days, with preliminary periods ranging from 2 to 16 days in length. The amount of protein in the rations was kept constant while the fat was increased from .297 kilograms to 1.706 kilograms per head daily. They found that the feeding of such large amounts of fat increased the percentage of fat in the milk, but reduced the yield so much as to make such feeding unprofitable.

Kellner and Andrä‡ compared sugar beets with dried and ensiled beet diffusion residue by feeding them alternately to twenty-four cows during four periods of twenty days each. They found that "the substitution of 4.4 kg. of dried diffusion residue for 27.5 kg. of sugar beets increased the milk yield .953 kg. and the substitution of 41.8 kg. of ensiled diffusion residue for the above amount of sugar beets increased the milk yield 1.721 kg. per cow (of 550 kg. live weight) without causing any material change in the quality of the milk."

Friis‖ reviews the coöperative cow feeding experiments conducted by the Experiment Station at Copenhagen, Denmark, since 1888, with especial reference to the effect of food on the fat content of the milk. The summary of 76 series of experiments is given. The rations used were such as could be regarded normal for milch cows, such as are met with in the feeding prac-

---

* Zeitschrift Physiol. Chem. 24 (1898) p. 425.

† Landwirtschaftliche Jahrbücher 27 (1898) p. 188.

‡ Landwirtschaftliche Versuchs Stationen 49 (1898) p. 402.

‖ Abs. in Experiment Station Record 10 (1898) p. 86, by F. W. Woll.

tice on Danish dairy farms. The question whether abnormal feed mixtures can appreciably change the fat content of milk was not included in the investigation. The author says "it was found that different feeding stuffs and food mixtures in a very large measure influence the quantity of milk yielded as well as the health and general condition of the cows. The feed under practical conditions as found in this country, exerts an entirely insignificant influence on the fat content of the milk."

Rhodin[*] emulsified linseed oil is a specially constructed machine and fed from 250 to 750 grams of the emulsion daily as a drink in water to each of two cows during seven-day periods in addition to a normal mixed ration. During the first periods of feeding the oil, the fat content of the milk was increased, but during the third period the per cent of fat not only ceased to increase, but fell back to the same point as before the oil was was fed.

Ramm and Winthrop[†] made a comparison of some new feeding stuffs using five cows for six months. The foods were corn bran, cocoa-molasses (hot molasses and finely ground cocoa shells), blood, molasses (blood, molasses and refuse of cereals) and molasses distillery refuse (residue from manufacture of alcohol from beet molasses). They found a wide fluctuation in the fat content of the milk during different periods and believe that the molasses increased the fat content wherever it was fed, while the corn bran seemed to reduce the fat content. When feeding rations rich in fat they could see no relation between the fat content of the ration and the fat content of the milk.

Ramm and Momsen[‡] report an experiment in which five cows were fed for four periods of four days each (preceded by preliminary periods) a basal ration of hay, straw, roots and peanut meal. In addition, molasses was fed during the first and fourth periods, raw sugar during the second period, and raw sugar and molasses distillery residue during the third period,—the sugar content of the three rations being the same. The cows produced the most milk and the least butter fat when fed the

---

[*] Milch Zeitung 27 (1898) pp. 306 and 323.
[†] Same, 27 (1898) p. 513.
[‡] Same, 29 (1900) 28, p. 433.

sugar ration, and the most fat and solids when fed the sugar and
molasses distillery residue.   The content of fat and solids in the
milk produced on the molasses ration was respectively, 3.20 and
11.65 per cent, on the sugar ration 2.84, and 11.32 per cent, and
on the sugar and molasses residue ration 3.39 and 12.06 per cent.
The results are therefore considered as showing that molasses
has a greater feeding value for dairy cows than sugar, and that
the constituents in molasses other than sugar are especially valuable in the production of butter fat.

Hagemann * conducted some experiments to determine whether
a fat rich fodder produces a fat rich milk.   During five periods,
varying in length from 21 to 35 days, he fed two cows on rations
containing from 175 to 720 grams of fat.   In addition to a basal
ration the grains added were corn meal, linseed-oil meal, malt
sprouts and peanut cake mixed with cocoa molasses.   In the
sixth period of seven days he gave 1.1 pounds of sesame oil to
each cow daily as an emulsion in drinking water.   He concludes
that " the proportional and absolute fat content of milk is not
dependent upon the amount of fat in the food."

The reports of forty-nine separate experiments have been herein
reviewed.   They may be classified in the following manner in
answering to the question : Was the percentage of fat in the
milk increased by the food given the cows ?

.	Yes.	No.	A tendency to increase
Feeding fat...	6	8	1
Feeding protein and mixed foods................	3	22	3
Feeding watery foods	—	2	—
Feeding molasses preparations	4	—	—
Total...........	13	32	4

Of the six experiments where the fat in the food increased the
proportion of milk-fat, one reports so great a reduction in the
yield as to make such feeding unprofitable.   The noted experiment of Soxhlet whereby he increased the per cent of milk-fat
by feeding the cows oil emulsified in the drinking water, has
been repeated many times by other experimenters, but only one
of them, so far as we know, has reached a similar result.   The

* Landwirtschaftliche Jahrbücher 28 (1899) p. 485.

protein foods which increased the per cent of fat were palm-nut meal and sugar meal.   The molasses preparations may owe their power to increase the fat content of milk to their rather abnormal character.

EXPERIMENTS AT CORNELL UNIVERSITY

These experiments were conducted for the purpose of determining the comparative effect of rations having different nutritive ratios upon milk production.   This question has been the subject of experimentation at various times and places as has been already noticed, but further investigation along possibly different lines may throw more light upon the problem.   Much discussion has occurred over the matter of the length of time during which a particular food should be tested and as to the accuracy of conclusions drawn from feeding trials where two or more foods were given during brief alternating periods.   Some contend that four or five weeks is sufficient time in which to secure the true effect of a food, some think that a shorter time, even ten days, is enough, while others hold that the longer the period the more accurate and conclusive the result.   It is well known that, when a radical change is made in the food of a cow, the secretion of milk is greatly affected.   This is most apparent in the fat content, which may either rise or fall, but is more apt to rise.   How long the fluctuation may continue depends upon the ability of the cow to accustom herself to the new feed, which time may be only a few days or it may be weeks.   And when the cow has become accustomed to the changed feed, her milk falls back to its normal average composition.   However, if the experiment is concluded before this time, or if the feed is again changed, then conclusions drawn therefrom must be more or less warped.

In order that these sources of error might be obviated, these experiments were not only continued for a long period, but no changes were made in the kinds of foods given during the whole time.   The feeding trials lasted through two successive winters and for a period of twenty-two weeks during each winter.   The effect of the different rations was studied by comparing the influence of each upon the average milk production of the cows used.   We think this method to be satisfactory because, in the first place, the cows were so selected as to make the different lots fairly equal as to age, breed and general characteristics : and in the second place, if a given ration will produce any particular effect upon milk production, then this ration will show its influence on the average composition of the milk from the lot of cows to which it is fed when compared with the average composition of milk from other cows on other rations.

This study is confined to the yield of milk and its quality so far as represented by the percentage of butter-fat. The determinations of fat were made by the Babcock test from samples of milk taken from each cow during the last three days of each week. These daily samples were tested separately and their average taken for the average per cent of fat in the week's milk. Each cow's milk was weighed as soon as drawn and the weekly yield of milk multiplied by the average per cent of fat gives the total fat produced during the week.

The rations fed were of three kinds, one with a narrow, one with a medium, and the third with a wide nutritive ratio. No analyses of foods were made except of the oat chop which was fed during the first year. The amount of dry substance and the nutritive ratio were calculated largely from the average composition of feeding stuffs given in Bulletin No. 11 of the Office of Experiment Stations.

With one exception the same cows were used throughout the two years of experiment. Moreover the same cows were fed rations having practically the same nutritive ratio though made up of different foods during both years, i. e. the cows receiving a narrow ration the first year also received a narrow ration the second year and likewise with the cows on other rations. None of the rations are what would be called unusual, for similar ones may be found in use on dairy farms in various parts of the country. During the whole length of both experiments it was the aim to give the cows all the food they could readily consume.

The records as published contain only the average data obtained from each lot of cows. In work of this kind, the average record of several cows is of more value than individual records taken singly, and it is from the average record that conclusions must be drawn. For this reason and in order to eliminate many long tables from these pages, the individual records are not published.

THE FIRST EXPERIMENT, 1895–6.

This feeding trial began Nov. 6, 1895, and continued for twenty-two weeks until Apr. 7, 1896. It was conducted by James M. Johnson then a graduate student in the College of Agriculture. The names of the cows used are given below together with their breed, age, number of days in milk and weight.

Name and breed.	Age.	Number of days in milk.	Weight beginning.	Weight end.	Gain.
LOT A :					
Garnet Valentine A.J.C.C.,73873	4	67	873	922	119
Belva 2d, ⅛ Holstein	2	49	891	1088	197
Julia, ⅞ Holstein	4	25	1196	1370	174
LOT B :					
Cherry, grade Jersey..........	2	49	721	849	128
Dora, ⅛ Holstein.............	4	62	1146	1213	67
Glista 4th H. F. H. B., 31408..	3	65	1064	1239	175
LOT C :					
Clara, grade Jersey	3	65	922	1063	141
Glista Netherland, H.F.H.B..					
32442......................	3	16	1038	1127	89
May 2d, ⅞ Holstein...........	3	54	1017	1223	206

The daily rations of the cows in each lot were made up as follows :

LOT A :
Grain mixture ....8 to 13 pounds.
    Gluten feed .... 3 parts.
    Oat chop. ....2 parts.
    Cottonseed meal.... ....2 parts.
    Linseed oil meal. ....1 part.
Corn silage ....40 to 45 pounds.
Clover hay...................................8 to 10 pounds.
Nutritive ratio 1:4.5
LOT B :
Grain Mixture ....8 to 10 pounds.
    Gluten feed ....2 parts.
    Oat chop...................................3 parts.
    Corn meal....................................1 part.
    Linseed oil meal ....1 part.
Corn silage .... 35 to 45 pounds.
Clover hay.................................. 4 to 10 pounds.
Nutritive ratio.. ....1:6
LOT C :
Grain mixture ....8 to 10 pounds.
    Oat chop...................................4 parts.
    Corn meal...................................4 parts.
    Linseed oil meal........................1 part.
Corn silage .... 35 to 40 pounds.
Timothy hay .... 4 to 8 pounds.
Nutritive ratio...1:9

Calculating each of these rations on the basis of 8 pounds of grain, 8 pounds of hay and 40 pounds of silage, each cow would receive the following number of pounds of digestible nutrients per day :

	Protein.	Carbo-hydrates.	Fat.	Nutritive ratio.
Lot A, narrow ration.........	2.90	10.78	1.09	1:4.5
Lot B, medium ration	2.25	11.61	.91	1:6.0
Lot C, wide ration...........	1.60	12.68	.75	1.9.0

Beginning with Dec. 14, each cow received 5 pounds of mangel-wurtzels per day in addition to the above rations.

Table I contains the average record of consumption of food and production of milk and fat for each of the three lots of cows named above. The data given includes the weekly average consumption of dry matter per head, the average daily consumption per 1000 pounds live weight, the nutritive ratio, the average weekly yield of milk and fat and the average per cent of fat.

TABLE I—1895-6

AVERAGE RECORD OF LOT A. (NARROW RATION)

Week.	Dry matter consumed.			Weekly product of milk and fat. Average per head.		
	Per head weekly.	Per 1000 lbs. daily.	Nutritive Ratio.	Pounds of milk.	Per cent fat	Pounds of fat.
1	159.46	23.34	1:4.53	219.50	3.64	7.98
2	164.01	23.59	1:4.50	221.33	3.20	7.08
3	164 71	23.66	1:4.50	220 92	3.35	7.41
4	166.27	23.24	1:4.51	208.67	3.55	7.41
5	170.55	23.46	1:4.43	202.42	3.52	7.13
6	171.19	23.26	1:4.38	200.33	3.42	6.85
7	175 05	23.65	1:4.35	196.33	3.22	6.36
8	177.32	23.72	1:4 32	199.00	3.39	6.75
9	170.55	22.61	1:4.28	191.00	3.31	6.32
10	171.11	22.64	1 4.29	195.67	3.23	6.32
11	171.96	22.74	1:4.29	197.08	3.39	6.68
12	174.19	22.92	1:4.24	191.25	3.26	6.24
13	173.20	22.74	1:4.20	191.08	3.47	6.63
14	178.43	23.48	1:4.26	183.75	3.60	6.62
15	180.12	23.58	1:4.27	184.42	3.61	6.67
16	180.97	23.55	1:4 28	191.33	3.50	6.74
17	180.69	23.37	1:4.28	186.42	3.53	6 59
18	176.73	22.68	1:4.25	169.50	3.53	5.98
19	177.44	22.57	1:4.26	176.83	3.86	6 83
20	178.71	22.56	1:4.23	177.17	3.63	6.44
21	179 13	22.45	1:4.27	166.83	3.60	6.01
22	179.16	22.26	1:4.27	166.67	3.62	6.04

TABLE I—(*Continued*)
Average Record of Lot B. (Medium Ration)

Week.	Dry matter consumed.			Weekly product of milk and fat. Average per head		
	Per head weekly.	Per 1000 lbs. daily.	Nutritive ratio.	Pounds of milk.	Per cent fat.	Pounds of fat.
1	162.25	24.03	1:6.12	187.50	3.35	6.27
2	161.42	23.70	1:6.11	191.42	3.33	6.37
3	161.55	23.56	1:6.11	182.50	3 38	6.17
4	162.26	23.57	1:6.12	180.75	3.58	6.47
5	165.52	23.77	1:6.05	175.75	3.19	5.61
6	167.28	23.81	1:6.03	166.50	3.44	5.73
7	171.70	24.25	1:5.97	177.75	3.28	5.82
8	173.29	24.16	1:5.94	167.58	3.16	5.30
9	167.81	23.53	1:5.89	164.75	3.05	5.02
10	163.72	22.66	1:5.89	167.33	3.07	5.14
11	171.23	23.51	1:5.96	169.25	3 45	5.84
12	168.72	23.14	1:5.96	164.92	3.32	5.48
13	170.11	23.29	1:5.95	165.67	3.32	5.49
14	168.18	23.05	1:5.88	152.83	3.40	5.20
15	169.63	23.47	1:5.93	154.08	3.60	5.55
16	173.43	23.44	1:5.95	162.83	3.50	5.70
17	174.34	23.49	1:5.96	159.17	3.52	5.60
18	173.46	23.21	1:5.96	156.50	3.59	5.61
19	173.21	23.00	1:5.96	152.67	3.73	5.69
20	173.77	22.91	1:5.96	154.67	3.53	5.46
21	174.48	22.86	1:5.96	146.42	3.51	5.14
22	173.35	22.50	1:5.96	125.33	3.84	4.81

Average Record of Lot C. (Wide Ration)

Week.	Dry matter consumed.			Weekly product of milk and fat. Average per head.		
	Per head weekly.	Per 1000 lbs. daily.	Nutritive ratio.	Pounds of milk.	Per cent fat.	Pounds of fat.
1	150.20	21.56	1:8.79	180.83	3.31	5.99
2	149.62	21.28	1:8.78	177.92	3.20	5.69
3	145.43	20.52	1:8.73	173.83	3.54	6.16
4	146.73	20.49	1:8.73	166.75	3.55	5.92
5	151.28	20 95	1:8.65	162.00	3.37	5.46
6	147.63	20.35	1:8.43	152.67	3.43	5.24
7	150.14	20.50	1:8.30	164.25	3.08	5.06
8	147.16	19.93	1:8.19	164.92	3.22	5.31
9	148.75	20.07	1:8.22	145.25	3.74	5.43
10	146.44	19.62	1:8.18	154.92	3.25	5.03
11	151.65	20.17	1:8.27	154.25	3.30	5.08
12	146.15	19.33	1:8.16	153.42	3.31	5.08
13	147.62	19.45	1:8.21	153.67	3.37	5.18
14	146.49	19.21	1:8.19	147.75	3.21	4.75
15	147.31	19.27	1:8.19	143.17	3.60	5.15
16	154.39	20.16	1:8.33	146.83	3.45	5.07
17	156.13	20.33	1:8.36	146 33	3.29	4.82
18	156.13	20.29	1:8.36	142.75	3.52	5.02
19	157.72	20.33	1:8.39	139.92	3.87	5.42
20	158.73	20.26	1:8.41	141.67	3.58	5 07
21	160 76	20.32	1:8.45	136.50	3.65	4.98
22	161.01	20.56	1:8.46	135.33	3.63	4.91

THE SECOND EXPERIMENT, 1896–7

This feeding trial continued for twenty-two weeks from Nov. 11, 1896, to Apr. 13, 1897, and was conducted by the writer. The names of the cows used are given below together with their breed, age, number of days in milk and weight. It will be noticed that these cows are the same that were in the first experiment with the exception of Jennie 2d, in lot C who took the place of Glista Netherland.

Name and breed.	Age.	Number of days in milk.	Weight begin- ning.	Weight end.	Gain.
LOT A :					
Garnet Valentine, A.J.C.C.73873		74	920	1026	100
Belva 2d, ⅛ Holstein		50	1012	1200	188
Julia, ⅞ Holstein	5	62	1247	1333	106
LOT B :					
Cherry, grade Jersey	3	54 Calved Nov. 20	809	928	119
Dora, ⅛ Holstein.............	5		1181	1213	32
Glista 4th, H. F. H. B. 31408...	4	60	1137	1289	152
LOT C :					
Clara, grade Jersey...........	4	68 Calved Nov. 8	1030	1062	32
Jennie 2d, Jersey-Holstein.....	3		857	952	95
May 2d, ⅞ Holstein..........	4	44	1124	1191	67

The daily rations of the cows in each lot were made up as follows :

LOT A :
```
    Grain mixture.........................................8 to 12 pounds.
        Gluten feed.................................................3 parts.
        Cottonseed meal ...........................................2 parts.
        Wheat bran.................................................1 part.
    Corn silage........................................35 to 45 pounds.
    Clover hay........................................ ......6 to 12 pounds.
    Nutritive ratio ............................................1:4.3
```
LOT B :
```
    Grain mixture.........................................8 to 12 pounds.
        Gluten feed .........................................  .....2 parts.
        Corn meal....... .......... .................2 parts.
        Wheat bran........................... .. .............. 2 parts.
        Linseed oil meal.................. .. ................1 part.
    Corn silage ......................................35 to 45 pounds.
    Clover hay.........................................6 to 12 pounds.
    Nutritive ratio.............................................1:5.7
```
LOT C :
```
    Grain mixture.............. .............  .......8 to 11 pounds.
        Corn meal.................................................2 parts.
        Wheat bran ...................... ............ .........1 part.
    Corn silage ..........................................35 to 40 pounds.
    Timothy hay.........................................4 to 8 pounds.
    Nutritive ratio ...........................................1:9.3
```

Calculating each of these rations on the basis of 8 pounds of grain, 8 pounds of hay, and 40 pounds of silage, each cow would receive the following number of pounds of digestible nutrients per day.

	Protein.	Carbo-hydrates.	Fat.	Nutritive ratio.
Lot A, narrow ration........	3.08	10.63	1.13	1:4.3
Lot B, medium ration	2.37	11.67	.87	1:5.7
Lot C, wide ration..........	1.56	12.96	.67	1:9.3

Beginning with Jan. 6, each cow was fed five pounds of mangel-wurtzels per day, which amount was increased to 10 pounds in a few days and so continued until the close of the experiment.

Table II contains the average record of consumption of food and production of milk and fat for each of the three lots of cows named above. The data given includes the weekly average consumption of dry matter per head, the average daily consumption per 1000 pounds live weight, the nutritive ratio, the average weekly yield of milk and fat and average per cent of fat.

TABLE II—1896–7.
AVERAGE RECORD OF LOT A. (NARROW RATION.)

Week.	Dry matter consumed.			Weekly product of milk and fat. Average per head.		
	Per head weekly.	Per 1000 lbs. daily.	Nutritive ratio.	Pounds of milk.	Per cent fat.	Pounds of fat.
1	167.19	22.63	1:4.15	184.42	3.37	6.21
2	169.34	22.53	1:4.11	188.33	3.31	6.24
3	172.81	22.67	1:4.11	187.75	3.27	6.14
4	172.98	22.32	1:4.00	178.25	3.44	6.13
5	169.36	21.82	1:3.94	177.08	3.21	5.64
6	175.30	22.48	1:4.01	176.17	3.20	5.64
7	176.12	22.47	1:4.03	166.50	3.25	5.41
8	178.18	22.61	1:4.04	169.92	3.08	5.24
9	163.61	20.50	1:3.98	153.33	3.26	5.00
10	142.36	18.59	1:4.12	150.58	3.37	5.08
11	169.11	21.52	1:4.03	161.75	3.27	5.28
12	163.36	20.74	1:3.96	152.08	3.17	4.82
13	169.52	21.56	1:3.95	147.92	3.15	4.66
14	171.13	21.55	1:3.90	156.83	3.34	5.23
15	173.60	21.76	1:3.93	155.67	3.26	5.08
16	178.23	22.07	1:3.92	150.58	3.22	4.85
17	182.63	22.51	1:3.94	152.25	3.21	4.88
18	179.27	21.93	1:3.93	151.17	3.41	5.15
19	176.46	21.52	1:3.92	148.83	3.32	4.94
20	174.74	21.16	1:3.91	148.58	3.31	4.92
21	175.69	21.20	1:3.91	150.75	3.37	5.09
22	174.61	20.87	1:3.90	143.50	3.36	4.83

TABLE II—(*Continued*)

AVERAGE RECORD OF LOT B. (MEDIUM RATION)

Week.	Dry matter consumed.			Weekly product of milk and fat. Average per head.		
	Per head weekly.	Per 1000 lbs. daily.	Nutritive ratio.	Pounds of milk.	Per cent fat.	Pounds of fat.
1	*162.22	23.96	1:5.58	*182.75	3.67	6.72
2	*164.89	23.76	1:5.54	*189.25	4.04	7.64
3	*166.15	23.44	1:5.54	*181.75	3.83	6.97
4	164.90	21.87	1:5.59	221.08	3.84	8.50
5	169.20	22.42	1:5.53	227.33	3.43	7.79
6	164.48	21.80	1:5.54	195.17	3.98	7.77
7	170.53	22.53	1:5.56	204.25	3.63	7.42
8	175.99	23.20	1:5.59	214.92	3.34	7.19
9	177.14	23.37	1:5.94	217.42	3.42	7.42
10	180.81	23.87	1:5.93	216.16	3.36	7.26
11	176.58	23.32	1:5.46	210.33	3.51	7.38
12	166.01	21.85	1:5.42	201.50	3.40	6.89
13	175.91	23.27	1:5.47	204.58	3.47	7.09
14	178.59	23.14	1:5.46	207.08	3.51	7.27
15	184.10	23.92	1:5 47	215.92	3.50	7.55
16	186.78	24.03	1:5.47	205.17	3.57	7.33
17	186.35	23.75	1:5.47	208.42	3.43	7.16
18	186.92	23.73	1:5.47	214.42	3.45	7.39
19	182.40	23.09	1:5.46	209.00	3.65	7.63
20	181.98	22.94	1:5.46	208.33	3.41	7.11
21	181.27	22.76	1:5.46	202.25	3.62	7.33
22	181.55	22.65	1:5.46	199.83	3.55	7.09

AVERAGE RECORD OF LOT C. (WIDE RATION)

Week.	Dry matter consumed.			Weekly product of milk and fat. Average per head.		
	Per head weekly.	Per 1000 lbs. daily.	Nutritive ratio.	Pounds of milk.	Per cent fat.	Pounds of fat.
1	*129.38	17.37	1:8.87	*179.75	3.63	6.53
2	141.92	20.56	1:9.02	189.08	3.96	7.49
3	147.75	21.21	1:8.99	186.25	3.95	7.36
4	144.32	20.71	1:8.95	174.17	4.09	7.12
5	135.80	19.52	1:8.79	169.92	3.89	6.61
6	149.93	21.48	1:9.08	169.33	3.78	6.39
7	153.89	21.97	1:9.12	156.75	3.63	6.18
8	156.10	22.23	1:9.15	169.42	3.73	6.32
9	155.15	22.12	1:8.90	167.50	3.99	6.68
10	158.99	22.56	1:8.76	161.42	4.05	6.54
11	158.09	22.37	1:8.75	160.92	4.06	6.53
12	152.95	21.53	1:8.75	157.08	4.10	6.44
13	159.51	22.42	1:8.80	155.83	4.06	6.32
14	158.27	22.04	1:8.69	157.42	4.06	6.39
15	159.68	22.44	1:8.69	158.33	3.99	6.32
16	152.38	20.90	1:8.55	147.92	4.18	6.18
17	154 93	21.04	1:8.56	153.42	4.06	6.23
18	157.59	21.37	1:8.61	151.67	4.06	6.16
19	151.51	20.40	1:8 51	146.25	4.16	6.08
20	*160.50	21.62	1:8.53	*161.38	3.64	5.88

* Average for two cows.

Before entering upon any discussion of these records it is necessary to make a few explanations in order that a clear understanding of them may be obtained. The first experiment went through without any irregularities, or illness of the cows, sufficient to cause variations that should be noticed when drawing conclusions. But during the second experiment there were some irregularities that need to be noticed.

In lot A, Table II, Julia was taken sick during the ninth week of the test and for a few days her milk yield fell off nearly one-half. Her illness and slow recovery considerably reduced the average milk and fat yield as may be seen by a glance at the table.

In lot B, Dora did not enter the experiment until the fourth week and was then fresh in milk. She was giving from 40 to 50 pounds of milk daily, which amount increased the average yield, as is seen in Table II. During the sixth week she was "off feed" and her milk fell from 325 pounds during the fifth week to 232 pounds. At the same time her average per cent of fat was over one per cent higher than during the week previous, as well as during the following week. This explains the high average of 3.98 per cent during the sixth week. She quickly regained nearly her former flow and at the close of the experiment was averaging 42 pounds per day.

In lot C, Jennie calved Nov. 8 and entered the experiment the second week, fresh in milk. Her coming into this lot increased both the average yield of milk and the per cent of fat for the second and succeeding weeks. During the twentieth week, Clara, of lot C, was taken suddenly ill with high fever and died. Upon examination, she was found to have accumulations of fatty tissue in close proximity to the vital organs. During the twenty-first week, May, of lot C, was taken ill in a similar manner to Clara, but her life was saved. It will be remembered that the cows in this lot received a highly carbonaceous ration. The grain consisted of two parts, by weight, of corn meal and one part of wheat bran, while the silage was rich in corn and had been increased five pounds each about a month before the cows became sick. It may be that so highly carbonaceous a ration has a heating tendency upon the animal body. If this be the case, feeding the ration for so long a period, might, in its cumulative effects, result as disastrously as mentioned above.   Although Jennie 2d came through the experiment safely on the same ration, still, when the effect upon Clara and May is considered, we cannot help concluding that the ration is not a good one for long, continuous feeding.

To return to the study of the comparative effect of the three rations upon the yield and quality of milk, the results show that there is practically no difference between them so far as their effect on the percentage of fat is concerned.   In general, there is a gradual increase in the richness of the milk from the beginning of each experiment until the end, regardless of the kind of food.   An average of the per cents of fat for periods of four weeks each will present the fact more clearly, and such an average is given in tabular form below.   The first two weeks are omitted in striking the average in all cases.

	1895-6. Lot and kind of ration.			1896-7. Lot and kind of ration.		
	A Narrow. per cent fat.	B Medium. per cent fat.	C Wide. per cent fat.	A Narrow. per cent fat.	B Medium. per cent fat.	C Wide. per cent fat
1st four weeks....	3.46	3.40	3.47	3.29	3.77	3.93
2d four weeks....	3.29	3.14	3.32	3.24	3.44	3.85
3d four weeks....	3 44	3.37	3.27	3.23	3.47	4.07
4th four weeks....	3.54	3.55	3.47	3.28	3 49	4.07
5th four weeks....	3.68	3.65	3.68	3.34	3.56	—

An average of this kind balances the variations from week to week, and places the per cents of fat in a light where conclusions can be more readily drawn therefrom.   The reason for the high average during the first four weeks in lot B, year 1896–7, has already been indicated in the discussion concerning Dora's entering the experiment when fresh in milk, and later becoming reduced in flow and increased in fat by forced feeding.   Omitting this period, it will be noticed that the average for the remaining periods bear the same relation to each other as those for lot A. In the first experiment there was an increase from the beginning to the end with each lot of about two-tenths of one per cent of fat.   In the second experiment this increase was about one-tenth of one per cent.

When we examine the yield of milk and of fat we do not find the same uniformity as is observed in the per cent of fat. If an average be taken of the yield of milk and fat for the first four weeks after the first two, and for the last four weeks of the experiments we find the following per cent of decrease from beginning to end :

	1895–6. Lot and kind of ration.			1896–7. Lot and kind of ration.		
	A Narrow.	B Medium.	C Wide.	A Narrow.	B Medium.	C Wide.
Per cent decrease in milk	17.5	18.0	15.5	17.8	3.0	14.4
Per cent decrease in fat	12.0	12.0	12.0	15.6	6.0	10.3

The decrease for 1895–6 was the same with all rations except for a slight difference in favor of the cows receiving the wide ration. During the year 1896–7 the yields are not so uniform, but lot B shows a much smaller decrease than either of the other lots. Taking both experiments into account it would seem that the medium ration had a more favorable influence upon the continued production of milk and total butter-fat than either the wide or narrow rations. Yet, if individual cases are considered, we find Belva 2d, on the narrow ration, holding out in her milk flow during both years as well as, or better than, any of the cows on the medium ration.

NUMBER OF POUNDS OF DRY MATTER REQUIRED IN EACH RATION TO PRODUCE 100 POUNDS OF MILK AND ONE POUND OF FAT

	LOT A. Narrow ration.		LOT B. Medium ration.		LOT C. Wide ration.	
	Milk.	Fat.	Milk.	Fat.	Milk.	Fat.
1895–6	90.2	26.0	102.8	30.1	98.3	28.7
1896–7	106.6	32.3	85.2	23.9	92.8	23.4
Average	97.5	28.8	93.0	26.6	95.7	25.9

WEIGHT OF COWS

Whether or not the different rations had any particular effect upon the live weight of the cows may be studied by recourse to data already given, but an average of the gain of each lot during the twenty-two weeks together with their average age is tabulated here, for more ready reference. During the first year none of the cows had reached full age and during the second year two of lot A and one of lot B were five years old. Since the cows in lot A were older than the others, it might seem that the nar-

	LOT A. Narrow ration.		LOT B. Medium ration.		LOT C. Wide ration.	
	Age.	Gain per head.	Age.	Gain per head.	Age.	Gain per head.
1896–6............	3⅓	163	3	123	3	145
1896–7............	4⅓	131	4	101	3⅔	65

row ration had a tendency to fatten the animals more than the other rations. However, the differences are so slight that it is safe to say that the gains in weight are due more to growth than to any particular effect of the food.

CHARTS

The records for milk and fat production as given in Tables I and II are shown diagramatically in the six charts immediately following. They show the average daily yield of milk, average per cent of fat and average weekly yield of fat for both experiments. Passing from left to right in the charts each division represents one week. Counting upward, each of the small spaces represents one-half pound of milk, five one-hundredths of one per cent fat, or one-tenth of a pound of fat as the case may be.

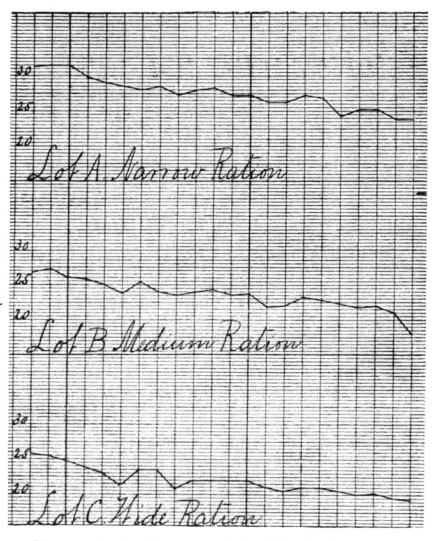

1.— *Diagram showing the average daily yield of milk for each week during the experiment of 1895-6. Each space between the perpendicular lines represents one week. Each space between the horizontal lines represents one-half pound of milk.*

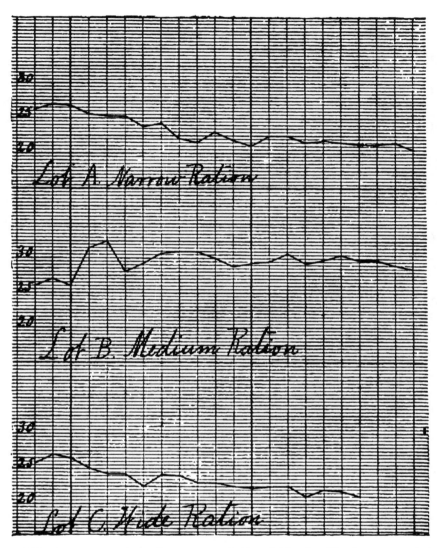

2.—Diagram showing the average daily yield of milk for each week during the experiment of 1896–7. Each space between the perpendicular lines represents one week. Each space between the horizontal lines represents one-half pound of milk.

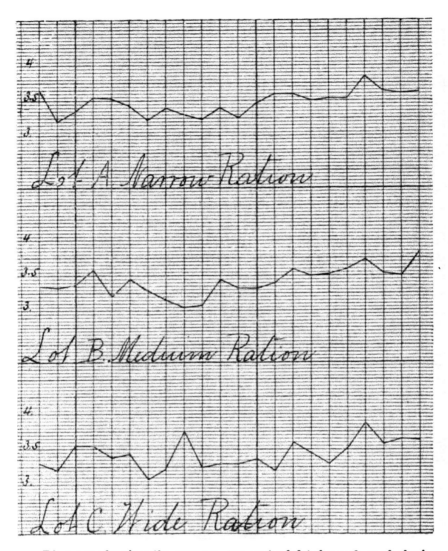

3.—*Diagram showing the average per cent of fat for each week during the experiment of 1895-6. Each space between the perpendicular lines represents one week. Each space between the horizontal lines represents five one-hundredths of one per cent of fat.*

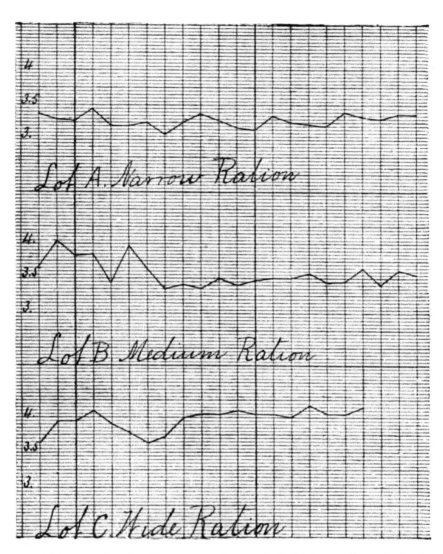

4.—Diagram showing the average per cent of fat for each week during the experiment of 1896-7. Each space between the perpendicular lines represents one week. Each space between the horizontal lines represents five one-hundredths of one per cent of fat.

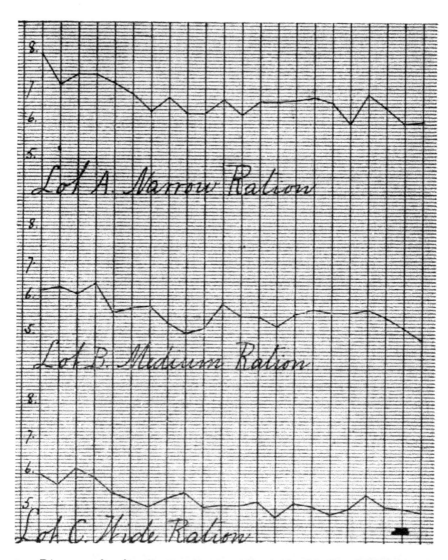

5.—Diagram showing the average weekly yield of butter fat during the experiment of 1895-6. Each space between the perpendicular lines represents one week. Each space between the horizontal lines represents one-tenth of one pound of fat.

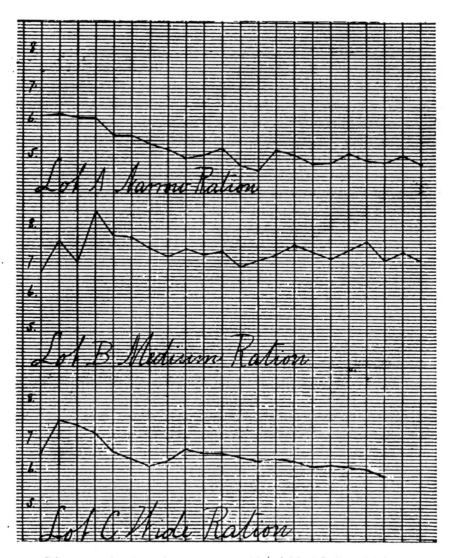

6.—*Diagram showing the average weekly yield of butter fat during the experiment of 1896-7. Each space between the perpendicular lines represents one week. Each space between the horizontal lines represents one-tenth of one pound of fat.*

FEEDING PALM NUT MEAL

To carry still further the study of the effect of food upon milk production a trial was made with palm nut meal.   This work was carried on during the winter of 1897 by George N. Lauman, then a Senior in the College of Agriculture.   An experiment with this food has a double interest because it is the one that Kühn found would increase the per cent of fat in the milk as has been seen in the summary of his work on page 26.

Palm nut meal is the by-product resulting from the extraction of the oil from the fruit of a species of palms which are native to the west coast of Africa.   It is a highly nitrogenous product, its percentage of digestible composition being protein 16.6, fiber 16.6, nitrogen free extract 41.4 and fat 3.6.   In Europe, and especially Germany, it has long been a popular dairy food because of its stimulative effect upon milk production, although not all feeders and experimenters have found it to increase the fat content of the milk as was reported by Kühn.

The meal used in this experiment was imported from Germany. Six of the University cows were chosen for the test and divided into two lots of three each.   Before giving them the palm nut meal, their regular daily ration had consisted of from 8 to 10 pounds of a grain mixture composed of three parts gluten feed, two parts cottonseed meal, and one part wheat bran, together with what silage and mixed hay they would eat.

The names of the cows in each lot, together with their age, date of calving and weights are given below :

Name of breed.	Age.	Date of calving.	Weight beginning.	Weight end.	Loss.
LOT NO. 1.					
Glista Netherland, H. F. H. B. 32442	5	Oct. 21, 1895.	1339	1289	50
Gem Valentine, A. J. C. C. 57881....	8	Sept. 6, 1896.	1071	973	98
Mollie, ⅛ Holstein..............	7	Oct. 24, 1896.	1348	1267	81
LOT NO. 2.					
Mabel 2d, Jersey Holstein..........	2	Oct. 15, 1896.	902	832	70
Ruby, ¼ Holstein..................	8	Dec. 26, 1896.	1369	1191	178
Sadie, ⅛ Holstein..........	5	May 1, 1896.	1407	1386	21

The feeding of the palm nut meal began Jan. 20, 1897, and continued for six weeks. During this time the ration of lot No. 1 remained constant, while that of lot No. 2 was increased as indicated below. The daily rations were made up as follows :

LOT No 1 :
Grain mixture..................................... .....10 to 13 pounds
    Palm nut meal..... .... 2 parts.
    Gluten feed... 2 parts.
    Wheat bran.......... .... 1 part.
Corn silage.............. ....35 to 45 pounds.
Mixed hay ....10 to 13 pounds.
Nutritive ratio...1:6

Calculating this ration on the basis of 10 pounds of grain, 10 pounds of hay and 40 pounds of silage it would contain the following number of pounds of digestible nutrients : protein 2.7 carbohydrates 14.1, fat .96 and 26 pounds of dry substance.

LOT No 2 :
Grain mixture
    Palm nut meal ....4 parts.
    Gluten feed ....3 parts.
    Cottonseed meal ....2 parts.
    Wheat bran ....1 part.
Corn silage ....35 to 45 pounds.
Mixed hay.................................... ...7 to 10 pounds.

The amount of coarse fodder given this lot did not vary materially during the whole experiment. The quantity of the grain mixture fed was increased as follows :

	January. 20–31.	February. 1–6.	February. 7–28.
Mabel..............	7	8.5	10
Ruby..............	10	12	14
Sadie	10	12	14

Calculating this ration according to the quantities eaten by Ruby and Sadie, and considering the amount of silage and hay consumed as 40 and 10 pounds respectively, we have the following amounts of dry matter and the number of pounds of digestible nutrients consumed daily during the different periods :

	Dry matter.		Protein.	Carbo-hydrates.	Fat.	Nutritive ratio.
	Per head.	Per 1000 lbs.				
January 20–31..	26.06	20.00	3 09	13.52	1.08	1:5.16
February 1–6...	27.87	21.51	3.52	14.42	1.22	1:4.84
February 7–28..	29.68	22.83	3.96	15.32	1.35	1:4.64

On Feb. 24 the proportion of palm nut meal was increased from four to six parts in the grain mixture so that it made up one-half of the grain ration. On the first of March the meal was discontinued and all the cows returned to the same ration which they received before the trial.

Table III contains the yield of milk and butter-fat of each cow under experiment for six weeks before and six weeks after the palm nut meal was fed as well as during the period of feeding the meal.

TABLE III
WEEKLY PRODUCT OF MILK AND FAT OF LOT NO. 1

Ration for each period of six weeks.	Glista Netherland.			Gem Valentine.			Mollie.		
	Pounds of milk.	Per cent fat.	Pounds of fat.	Pounds of milk.	Per cent fat.	Pounds of fat	Pounds of milk.	Per cent fat.	Pounds of fat.
Usual ration of silage, hay and grain.	204.25	3.00	6.13	157.00	5.20	8.16	334.25	2.60	8.69
	217.50	3.15	6.85	176.50	5.30	9.35	347.50	2.95	10.25
	207.50	3.00	6.23	145.50	5.35	7.78	321.50	3.40	10.93
	211.00	3.25	6.86	116.00	4.85	5.63	313.50	3.00	9.41
	202.75	3.25	6.59	118.50	4.85	5.75	305.50	2.65	8.10
	201.50	3.50	7.05	131.25	5.50	7.22	299.50	3.10	9.28
Total	1244.50	3.19	39.71	844.75	5.20	43.89	1921.75	2.95	56.66
Palm nut meal ration.	206.50	3.20	6.61	127.75	5.52	7.05	311.00	3.17	9.86
	196.50	3.38	6.64	123.25	5.88	7.25	293.50	3.26	9.57
	182.25	3.41	6.21	122.75	6.00	7.37	295.25	3.38	9.98
	187.00	3.75	7.01	117.75	5.98	7.04	296.75	3.48	10.33
	184.00	3.48	6.40	117.50	5.57	6.54	298.75	3.35	10 01
	164.75	3.75	6.18	105.50	5.85	6.17	295.00	3.53	10.41
Total	1121.00	3.48	39.05	714.50	5.80	41.42	1790.25	3.36	60.16
Usual ration.	139.50	3.42	4.77	111.50	5.73	6.36	285.50	3.07	8.76
	*62.00	3.60	2.23	114.75	6.00	6.89	315.50	3.30	10.41
				108.00	5.65	6.10	304.00	3.55	10.79
				83.75	5.95	4.98	307.75	3.25	10.00
				93.25	5.75	5.36	294.00	3.40	10.00
				93.75	5.85	5.48	290.75	3.25	9.45
Total	201.50	3.47	7.00	605.00	5.82	35.20	1797.50	3.31	59.14

* Went dry.

TABLE III (*Continued*)

WEEKLY PRODUCT OF MILK AND FAT OF LOT No. 2

Ration for each period of six weeks.	Mabel 2d.			Ruby.			Sadie.		
	Pounds of milk.	Per cent fat.	Pounds of fat.	Pounds of milk.	Per cent fat.	Pounds of fat.	Pounds of milk.	Per cent fat.	Pounds of fat.
Usual ration of silage, hay and grain.	183.75	3.90	7.17				169.75	3.20	5.43
	186.25	4.10	7.64				163.50	3.05	4.99
	163.25	3.80	6.20				147.00	3.40	5.00
	167.50	3.95	6.62	336.25	3.75	12.61	141.25	3.60	5.09
	176.00	3.90	6.86	385.25	3.80	14.64	148.00	3.45	5.11
	171.00	3.45	5.90	408.00	3.50	14.28	144.50	3.90	5 64
Total	1047.75	3.85	40.39	1129.50	3.67	41.53	914.00	3.42	31.26
Palm nut meal ration.	160.25	4.07	6.52	434.25	3.26	14.16	132.25	3.22	4.26
	148.75	4.58	6.81	439.00	3.28	14.40	119.75	3.28	3.93
	150.75	4.33	6.53	418.75	3.25	13.61	119.50	3.33	3.98
	152.00	4.53	6.89	423.25	3.26	13.80	122.50	4.06	4.97
	148.75	4.35	6.47	422.25	3.21	13.55	122.75	3.23	3.96
	149.50	4.18	6.25	415.75	3.35	13.93	113.75	3.46	3.94
Total	910.00	4.34	39.47	2553.25	3.27	83.45	730 50	3.43	25.04
Usual ration.	162.25	3.69	5.99	409.50	3.00	12.29	104.25	3.12	3.25
	169.75	3.80	6.45	389.50	3.20	12.75	104.75	2.30	2.41
	170.50	3 85	6.56	422.75	2.80	11.84	97.75	3.40	3.32
	171.00	4.00	6.84	397.50	3.25	12.92	86.75	3.30	2 86
	173.25	4.35	7.54	374.25	3.25	12.16	77.50	3.70	2.87
	174.00	3.75	6.53	345.50	2.90	10.02	67.25	3.45	2.32
Total	1020.75	3.91	39.91	2348.00	3.07	71.98	538.25	3.16	17.03

A clearer understanding of the variations in the per cent of fat during the eighteen weeks may be obtained by finding the average per cent in periods of three weeks each. A table of such averages is given below. In order to make the study more complete, there is placed in the same table the average per cents of fat found in the records of three cows which were in the second experiment described on page 38. The per cents are the averages for the periods of three weeks each which are coincident with those in which palm nut meal was fed. It will be remembered that the rations of the three cows were unaltered during a term of twenty-two weeks.

TABLE IV

AVERAGE PER CENT OF FAT IN PERIODS OF THREE WEEKS EACH

		Lot No. 1.			Lot No. 2.		
		Glista Netherland.	Gem Valentine.	Mollie.	Mabel 2d.	Ruby.	Sadie.
Usual ration (Dec. 9–Jan. 19)...	1st three weeks.	3.06	5.28	2.98	3.94	—	3.21
	2d three weeks.	3.39	5.09	2.92	3.77	3 67	3.63
Palm nut meal ration.......... (Jan. 20–Mar. 2).	1st three weeks	3.32	5.80	3.27	4.32	3.26	3.28
	2d three weeks.	3.64	5.80	3.45	4.35	3.27	3.58
Usual ration (Mar. 3–Apr. 13)..	1st three weeks.	3.47	5.80	3.31	3.78	3.00	2 92
	2d three weeks.	—	5.84	3.30	4.03	3.14	3.48

Ration unchanged.	Belva 2d. Narrow ration.	Cherry Medium ration.	Clara. Wide ration.
Dec. 9–29	3.02	5.37	5.11
Dec. 30–Jan. 19................	2.92	5.58	5.30
Jan. 20–Feb. 9................	2.94	5.75	5.68
Feb. 10–Mar. 2	3 14	5.52	5.44
Mar. 3–23.....................	3.23	5.55	5.45
Mar. 24–Apr. 13..	3.23	5.47	—

Among the cows that were fed palm nut meal it is seen that all in lot No. 1 show in general a higher per cent of fat while the meal was fed than before, but this higher average is kept up for six weeks after the meal was discontinued. Mabel 2d of lot No. 2, is the only cow that shows a lower average both before and after feeding the palm nut meal than during that period, but her total yield of fat was less on the palm nut ration than on the usual ration. Ruby and Sadie each had a higher average before the meal was fed and nearly as high after as during the period of feeding the meal. Ruby's high average at the beginning is probably due to her being fresh in milk. A comparison of the records of all the cows in Table IV shows that with one exception (Gem Valentine) there are no greater variations among the cows which alternated from the usual ration to palm nut meal than among those which were fed an unchanging ration. Thus, taking everything into consideration we do not feel warranted in saying that the feeding of palm nut meal increased the per cent of fat in the milk.

RELATION OF THE TEMPERATURE OF THE COW
TO THE SECRETION OF MILK FAT

Among the many theories concerning the cause of the variations in the percentage of fat in the milk of a single cow is the notion that the temperature of the animal body may be a governing factor in such variation. This idea may have found its origin in the statement from some sources that a cow when in a feverish condition is likely to give milk containing a proportion of butter-fat higher than the normal content of her milk. The inference might be that under ordinary conditions the variation which is found in the per cent of fat from one milking to the next might be accompanied by a corresponding rise-or fall in animal heat. In order to secure some experimental data upon this question, a series of records was gathered along three lines: One in which the record period comprises five days immediately preceding and following the oestrum day of several cows and in which the temperature of the cow was taken at the time of each milking. A second in which is included the record of-two cows which were spayed and the temperatures were taken four times daily, i.e. at the time of, and eight hours ·previous to milking. And a third in which an attempt was made to find the average temperature of each cow for the entire day by taking the temperature at intervals of four hours. It is well known that an animal's temperature varies somewhat and it was thought possible to obtain the more exact temperature of the cow during the time in which her milk was secreted by recording her temperature at frequent intervals.

The cows from which the records were obtained were members of the Cornell University dairy herd. They were fed the usual stable ration of about eight pounds of mixed grain daily, seven to twelve pounds of mixed clover and timothy hay and as much corn silage as they would consume at a single feed. They were fed twice daily and were usually kept in the stable only for milking and feeding and, during the remainder of the night and day, were in a covered yard. A watering place was provided in the yard and no water was given in the stable. The cows were

milked at five o'clock in the morning and at four in the afternoon. This divided the time so that there were thirteen hours
between night and morning and eleven hours between morning
and night milkings. The difference in the interim accounts for
the larger amount of milk being usually given in the morning

The series of records as outlined is given in the following
table. The study of the influence of oestrum is set forth in the
records of eleven cows covering seventeen different periods of
eleven days each. The oestrum day is indicated by the day of
the month being set opposite the data for that day. The other
days are indicated by numbers from one to five consecutively
before and after the initial day. So far as could be detected
from outward appearances, the period of oestrum seemed to be
confined to twenty-four hours. The records appear in Table V,
wherein are given the pounds of milk, per cent of fat, pounds of
fat and temperature of the cow at the time of milking.

The study of the influence of spaying upon milk secretion is
set forth in the records of two cows for thirteen days, i. e. six
days before and after the operation was performed. These
records are displayed in Table V, wherein are given the pounds
of milk, per cent of fat and pounds of fat secreted at each milking and also the temperature of the cow at milking time, eight
hours previous to milking and the average of the two temperatures.

The study of the constant temperature of the cow in its relation to milk secretion is set forth in Table V, wherein are given
the pounds of milk, per cent of fat and pounds of fat secreted
at each milking and also the temperature of the cow at milking,
four and eight hours previous to milking and the average of the
three temperatures.

TABLE V

RELATION OF TEMPERATURE OF COW TO THE SECRETION OF MILK FAT

I. Influence of Oestrum

INDIVIDUAL RECORDS OF MILK, FAT AND TEMPERATURE

	Days and dates, 1898.	Pounds of milk.		Per cent of fat.		Pounds of fat.		Temperature.	
		A.M.	P.M.	A.M.	P.M.	A.M.	P.M.	A.M.	P.M.
Ada.........	5	11.0	10.0	4.05	4.05	.446	.405	101.6	102.1
	4	11.0	9.8	4.30	4.65	.473	.456	101.8	103.0
	3	8.3	9.3	4.45	—	.369	—	102.0	102.4
	2	7.3	9.5	4.75	4.60	.347	.437	101.7	102.6
	1	11.3	10.5	4.00	3.85	.452	.404	102.0	103.3
	Nov. 1	11.0	11.3	4.55	3.65	.501	.412	102.4	102.4
	1	12.0	12.0	3.80	4.00	.456	.480	102.0	102.7
	2	11.8	11.0	3.75	3.45	.443	.380	101.7	102.0
	3	13.0	11.8	—	4.15	—	.490	101.3	102.8
	4	12.3	11.0	3.75	3.60	.461	.396	101.6	102.4
	5	12.8	10.8	4.00	4.00	.512	.432	102.4	—
Belle.........	5	18.5	17.3	3.65	5.70	.675	.986	101.5	102.0
	4	16.5	14.0	3.35	3.75	.553	.525	102.2	102.2
	3	15.3	15.0	4.20	3.70	.643	.555	102.2	101.7
	2	17.8	16.5	3.60	5.40	.641	.891	102.0	102.0
	1	21.3	15.8	—	5.00	—	.790	102.0	101.8
	Nov. 21	19.0	14.5	4.60	5.35	.874	.776	102.5	102.2
	1	17.0	17.0	4.00	5.00	.680	.850	102.0	102.7
	2	18.3	16.3	4.25	4.75	.778	.774	101.4	102.0
	3	19.3	15.8	4.35	4.90	.840	.774	101.0	102.0
	4	19.0	16.5	4.05	4.60	.770	.759	101.6	101.6
	5	19.3	16.3	4.20	4.55	.811	.752	101.6	102.2
Belva 2d......	5	19.3	18.8	2.75	4.20	.521	.790	101.6	101.0
	4	21.0	19.8	2.80	3.25	.588	.644	101.9	102.4
	3	18.3	17.5	3.00	4.00	.549	.700	102.6	102.0
	2	12.5	19.5	3.50	2.90	.438	.566	102.4	101.0
	1	20.3	21.8	2.70	3.50	.548	.763	102.0	102.0
	Nov. 14	21.0	21.3	2.55	—	.536	—	102.2	102.0
	1	21.5	21.8	3.35	3.55	.720	.774	102.2	102.5
	2	22.5	21.3	3.40	3.75	.765	.799	102.3	102.4
	3	21.8	21.0	3.10	3.10	.676	.651	103 0	102.8
	4	22.8	21.3	3.05	3.05	.695	.650	102.4	102.2
	5	20.3	20.8	2.80	3.20	.568	.666	103.0	102.7
Emma........	5	20.0	17.0	3.25	3.00	.650	.510	101.2	101.8
	4	22.5	17.3	3.15	2.75	.709	.475	101.5	101.6
	3	21.5	16.5	2.20	2.85	.473	.470	102.0	—
	2	23.3	18.8	3.30	3 80	.769	.714	101.3	101.8
	1	22.8	18.5	3.40	3.05	.775	.564	101.4	101.2
(1)	Nov. 9	21.8	17.5	2.75	3.00	.599	.525	101.3	101.8
	1	21.5	16.5	2.80	3.00	.602	.495	101.2	101.6
	2	20.3	16.3	2.60	3.00	.528	.489	101.6	102.0
	3	20.8	17.8	2.55	2.80	.530	.498	101.5	101.2
	4	21.3	16.0	2.60	2.80	.554	.448	101.6	101.6
	5	21.3	17.3	2.70	2.70	.575	.467	101.8	102.2

TABLE V—(*Continued*)

I. Influence of Oestrum

INDIVIDUAL RECORDS OF MILK, FAT AND TEMPERATURE

	Days and dates, 1898.	Pounds of milk.		Per cent of fat.		Pounds of fat.		Temperature.	
		A.M	P.M	A M.	P.M.	A.M.	P.M.	A.M.	P.M.
Emma.......	5	18.8	15.5	3.00	3.30	.564	.512	101.3	102.0
	4	18.0	13.8	2.85	3.00	.513	.514	101.8	101.8
	3	19.3	14.8	2.80	2.49	.540	.355	101.6	101.8
	2	17.5	17.3	2.35	3.40	.411	.588	101.4	101.2
	1	20 0	16.0	2.55	3.20	.510	.512	101.2	101.7
(2)	Dec. 1	19.3	15.8	2.65	2.90	.511	.458	101.4	·102.0
	1	18.3	14.8	2 90	2.95	.531	.437	104.0	101.4
	2	19.3	15.8	2.60	3.10	.502	.490	101.0	101.4
	3	20.0	15.0	2.80	2.90	.560	.435	101.3	101.4
	4	18.0	15.5	2.80	2.85	.504	.442	101.4	101.6
	5	19.3	16.0	2.60	2.90	.502	.464	101.5	101.3
Floss..	5	16.3	11.8	4.60	4.80	.750	.566	101.3	101.7
	4	14.0	12.5	4.20	—	.588	—	101.5	101.8
	3	15.8	12.3	5.00	5 40	.790	.664	101.0	101.4
	2	15.8	12.3	5.15	5.00	.814	.615	101.0	101.5
	1	14.5	12.0	4.65	5 75	.674	.690	100.8	101.8
	Oct. 26	14.3	10.8	4.90	4.60	.701	.497	101.6	102.0
	1	15.0	10.3	5.15	6.35	.773	.654	101.6	102.2
	2	13.5	11.3	5.45	6.00	.736	.678	101.6	101.3
	3	13.8	10.5	5.65	5.35	.780	.562	101.2	101.4
	4	*14.4	4.0	4.50	—	.648	—	103.1	101.3
	5	7.0	8.3	3.60	5.50	.252	.457	101.2	102.0
Ida.........	5	5 8	5.5	3.80	3.20	.220	.176	102.2	102.8
	4	7.3	6.3	2.90	3.55	.212	.224	102.0	101.8
	3	8.3	6.8	3.20	3.75	.266	.255	102.5	103.0
	2	8.8	6.8	3.40	3.70	.299	.252	103.8	103.0
	1	10.3	7.8	3.75	4.00	.386	.312	102.0	102.0
	Nov. 27	10.8	7.3	3.35	3.85	.362	.281	102.4	101.5
	1	11.3	8.3	3.75	3 75	.424	.311	102.2	102.0
	2	10.8	9.0	3.55	3.55	.363	.320	101.8	102.2
	3	12.0	9.3	3 40	3.45	.408	.321	101.8	102.0
	4	11.8	10 3	3.00	3.15	.354	.324	101.8	101.8
	5	12.5	10.0	3.35	3.10	.419	.310	102.0	102.0
Julia.	5	22.3	21.0	3.10	3.50	.691	.735	101.0	101.2
	4	22.3	19.0	3.65	3.70	.814	.703	100.8	101.8
	3	23 8	18 3	3.50	3.75	.833	.686	101.0	101.4
	2	22.0	20.8	2 80	4.20	.616	.874	100.7	101.4
	1	20.0	20.8	2.30	3.25	.460	.676	100.7	101.3
(1)	Oct. 19	16.8	24 8	1.55	4 75	.250	1.378	102.2	102.2
	1	21.3	16.5	4.25	3.55	.905	.586	101.0	101.7
	2	23.3	18.8	3 00	3.6)	.699	.677	101.3	101.6
	3	21.5	18.5	3.10	3.35	.667	.620	201.0	101.4
	4	23.5	16.8	2.85	3 85	.670	.647	101.6	102.8
	5	18 0	21.8	2.05	4 00	.369	.872	101.1	102.0

* One quarter of udder caked.

TABLE V—(*Continued*)

I. Influence of Oestrum

INDIVIDUAL RECORDS OF MILK, FAT AND TEMPERATURE

	Days and dates, 1898.	Pounds of milk.		Per cent of fat.		Pounds of fat.		Temperature.	
		A.M.	P.M.	A.M.	P.M	A.M.	P.M.	A.M.	P.M.
Julia	5	19.8	19.0	2.20	3.70	.436	.703	101.4	——
	4	20.8	19.0	2.50	3.65	.520	.694	101.3	101.7
	3	23.0	18.5	3.40	3.45	.782	.638	101.0	101.1
	2	19.8	16.8	2.85	3.20	.564	.538	101.0	100.0
	1	20.5	17.3	2.65	3 60	.543	.623	101.4	102.0
(2)	Nov. 11	13.8	15.5	2.75	3.65	.380	.566	103.1	101.6
	1	18.3	15.3	2.90	3.00	.532	.459	101.5	101.0
	2	18.5	14.0	2.70	3.30	.500	.462	101.5	101.8
	3	17.0	14.8	2.60	3.20	.442	.474	101.5	102.5
	4	16.0	15.3	2.85	3.35	.456	.513	101.8	102.0
	5	18.3	15.8	3.co	3.75	.549	.593	101.3	102.2
	5	18.5	16.0	3.00	3.20	.555	.512	101.6	101.6
	4	18 5	16.3	2.80	3.55	.518	.579	101.7	101.8
	3	19.3	15.0	2.80	3.00	.540	.450	101.4	102.0
	2	17.3	18.3	2.10	3.40	.363	.622	101.4	102.4
	1	21.3	18 5	2.90	3.65	.618	.675	101.2	101.7
(3)	Nov. 30	20.5	16.0	2.75	2.80	.564	.448	102.0	102.4
	1	19.5	16.5	3.15	3.co	.614	.495	101.4	101.7
	2	20.0	17.0	2.85	3.00	.570	.510	101.2	102.0
	3	20.3	16.8	2.80	3.35	.568	.563	101.8	101.8
	4	21.5	16.8	2.90	3.35	.624	.563	101.4	101.6
	5	19.0	16.8	2.90	3.10	.551	.521	101.4	101.6
Kate........	5								
	4	11.3	10.0	3.15	3.40	.356	.340	101.9	102.4
	3	11.0	9.5	2.80	3.05	.308	.290	101.4	101.8
	2	11.5	9.3	3.40	3.40	.391	.316	101.4	101.6
	1	11.8	8.5	3.20	3.40	.358	.293	101.5	101.6
(1)	Nov. 2	11.8	9.3	3.20	3.80	.358	.353	102.1	102.2
	1	10.8	9.3	3.20	3.55	.346	.330	102.3	102.4
	2	12.0	9.8	3.20	3.70	.384	.363	102.2	102.2
	3	12 3	10.0	3.15	3.70	.387	.370	101.8	102.5
	4	12.3	10.0	3.00	4.00	.369	.400	102.2	——
	5	12.3	9.3	3.10	3.80	.381	.353	101.4	101.5
	5								
	4	11.3	10.3	——	3.30	——	.340	101.7	102.6
	3	11.3	10 0	3.00	3.20	.339	.320	102.0	102.0
	2	11.0	9.0	2.80	2.80	.308	.252	102.0	101.4
	1	11.8	9.0	3.00	3.65	.354	.329	101.8	102.0
(2)	Nov. 21	10.3	8.5	3.40	4.00	.350	.340	102.2	102.3
	1	11.3	9.3	3.45	3 60	.390	.335	101.0	101.8
	2	11.5	9.5	3.45	3.25	.397	.309	101.6	102.3
	3	11.5	9.8	3.20	3.45	.368	.338	101.8	102.6
	4	11.8	9.3	3.25	3.40	.384	.316	101.6	102.4
	5	11.3	9.8	3.25	3.60	.397	.353	101.6	102.6

TABLE V—(*Continued*)

I. Influence of Oestrum

INDIVIDUAL RECORDS OF MILK, FAT AND TEMPERATURE

	Days and dates, 1898.	Pounds of milk.		Per cent of fat.		Pounds of fat.		Temperature.	
		A.M.	P.M.	A.M.	P.M.	A.M.	P.M.	A.M.	P.M.
Mabel 2d	5	11.0	9.8	3.80	4.00	.418	.392	101.4	101.7
	4	11.8	9.3	4.05	3.60	.478	.335	101.2	101.3
	3	10.5	11.3	2.70	4.15	.284	.467	101.0	101.8
	2	11 8	10.8	3.95	4.40	.466	.475	101.0	101.4
	1	11.3	10.0	3.55	4.10	.401	.410	101.0	101.8
(1)	Oct. 24	12.0	10.0	3.50	4.15	.420	.415	101.6	102.0
	1	12.3	10.3	4.55	4.15	.560	.427	100.8	102.3
	2	11.8	10.3	4.15	4.55	.490	.470	102.5	101.5
	3	11.5	8.5	—	4.25	- -	.361	101.8	103.8
	4	11.5	7.8	4.20	4.45	.483	.347	104.0	102.4
	5	10.0	8.8	—	4.00	—	.352	101.3	101.6
	5	*6.3	7.5	5.00	4.00	.315	.300	100.8	101.0
	4	12.3	9.5	4.80	3.85	.590	.366	101.9	102.0
	3	11.0	9.8	3.20	3.75	.352	.368	101.6	102.0
	2	10.0	11 3	3.00	3.65	.300	.412	101.6	101.0
	1	12.3	10.5	4.20	3.65	.517	.383	101.6	102.0
(2)	Nov. 14	12.3	9.5	3.50	4.00	.431	.380	101.8	101.4
	1	11.5	9 5	3.95	4.25	.454	.404	102.7	101.8
	2	11.8	9.8	4.10	4.35	.484	.426	101.5	101.6
	3	12.0	10.3	3.75	3.95	.450	.407	101.3	101.6
	4	12.3	10 0	3.90	3.75	.480	.375	101.4	102.0
	5	12.3	10.0	3.70	3.90	.457	.390	101.3	101.8
Ruby	5	19.3	22.3	3.95	3.90	.762	.870	101.3	101.8
	4	22.0	18.3	2.85	3.35	.627	.613	102.0	103.4
	3	18.3	18.3	3.00	2.85	.549	.525	102.0	101.5
	2	21.0	20.3	3.60	3.45	.806	.700	101.6	101.6
	1	22.8	18.8	3.25	3.50	.741	.658	101.8	—
(1)	Nov. 4	22.8	16.8	3.00	3.60	.684	.605	103.2	102.0
	1	22.0	18.5	3.40	3.25	.748	.601	102.2	101.4
	2	25.3	20.8	3.10	3.75	.784	.780	102.6	—
	3	24.8	21.5	2.80	3.70	.694	.796	101.8	101.8
	4	23.8	22.0	3.25	3.35	.774	.737	101.6	101.4
	5	23.3	21.3	3.05	3.55	.711	.756	101.7	100.8
	5	21.3	18.0	3.10	3.05	.660	.549	101.4	102.0
	4	22.8	17.0	3.20	3.05	.730	.519	102.0	102.2
	3	21.0	15.5	2.80	3.00	.588	.465	100.8	101.7
	2	18.5	18.0	2.8	2.80	.5 8	.504	101.2	101.8
	1	19 8	19.5	3.25	3.40	.644	.663	101.0	101.8
(2)	Nov. 24	21.3	17.5	3.55	3.75	.756	.656	100.8	101.2
	1	20.8	17.3	3.25	3.30	.676	.561	102.0	101.4
	2	21.0	19.0	3.20	3.55	.672	.675	101.0	101.6
	3	22.3	16.8	3.40	3.60	.758	.605	102.0	101.4
	4	22.3	18.8	3.30	3.40	.736	.639	101.4	101.6
	5	21.8	18.5	3.30	3.45	.719	.638	101.4	101.6

* Udder feverish and caked in one quarter.

TABLE V—(*Continued*)

I. Influence of Oestrum

INDIVIDUAL RECORDS OF MILK, FAT AND TEMPERATURE

	Days and dates, 1898.	Pounds of milk.		Per cent of fat		Pounds of fat.		Temperature.	
		A.M.	P.M.	A.M.	P.M.	A.M.	P.M.	A.M.	P.M.
Ruth	5	16.3	17.0	4.20	4.00	.685	.680	101.8	102.4
	4	17.5	15.0	3.60	4 30	.630	.645	102.3	102.3
	3	16.5	14.0	3.45	3.65	.560	.511	102.0	102.1
	2	15.8	13 3	3.45	4.40	.545	.585	105.4	102.0
	1	15.0	16.5	3.80	4.25	.570	.701	104.4	102.7
	Nov. 16	16.5	14.5	3.95	4.20	.652	.619	102.4	103.6
	1	15.3	15.8	3.90	3.70	.597	.585	102.2	101.8
	2	16.0	17.3	4.00	4.20	.640	.727	101.8	102.0
	3	16.3	16.0	3.60	3.05	.577	.488	101.8	103.5
	4	17.5	15.0	4.00	3.35	.700	.503	101.6	101.6
	5	16.5	16.3	3.40	3.35	.561	.546	101.0	102.0

II. Influence of Spaying

EMMA, (3)

INDIVIDUAL RECORDS OF MILK, FAT AND TEMPERATURE

Date, Nov., 1899	Time.	Pounds of milk.	Per cent of fat.	Pounds of fat.	Temperature.		
					8 hrs. before milking.	At time of milking	Average.
16	5 A.M.	22.2	2 6	.577	100.6	100.7	100.65
	4 P.M.	16.1	3.0	.483	101.4	101.5	101.45
17	5 A.M.	21.7	2.7	.606	100.6	101.0	100.80
	4 P.M.	15.8	2.9	.458	101.7	100.9	101.30
18	5 A.M.	22.2	2.5	.555	100.6	101.0	100.80
	4 P.M.	16.5	2.9	.479	101.4	100.9	101.15
19	5 A.M.	22.3	2.5	.558	101.4	101.2	101.30
	4 P.M.	16.3	2.8	.456	101.6	100.8	101.20
20	5 A.M.	22.1	2.6	.575	100.7	101.5	101.10
	4 P.M.	17.8	3.0	.534	101.5	102.0	101.75
21	5 A.M.	21.5	3.0	.645	101.3	101.5	101.40
	4 P.M.	16.7	2.6	.434	101.7	101.2	101.45
22	5 A.M.	21.7	2.6	.564	100.7	101.4	101.05
	*4 P.M.	15.1	3.5	.529	101.8	102.4	102.10
23	5 A.M.	10.2	4.9	.500	102.0	101.8	101.90
	4 P.M.	8.1	3.8	.308	102.4	103.2	102.80
24	5 A.M.	15.0	3.2	.480	101.9	101.2	101.55
	4 P.M.	13.5	3.4	.459	101.5	101.8	101.65
25	5 A.M.	17.7	2.9	.513	101.4	101.4	101.40
	4 P.M.	14.2	3.0	.426	101.5	101.6	101.55
26	5 A.M.	18.7	2.5	.468	101.0	101.4	101.20
	4 P.M.	15.2	3.0	.456	101.6	102.0	101.80
27	5 A.M.	17.3	2.5	.432	101.4	101.8	101.60
	4 P.M.	15.3	3.0	.459	101.9	101.9	101.90
28	5 A.M.	20 3	2.6	.528	101.6	101.6	101.60
	4 P.M.	14.9	3.0	.447	102.0	101.8	101.90

* Spayed at 2. P.M.

TABLE V—(*Continued*)
II. Influence of spaying
RUTH (2)
INDIVIDUAL RECORDS OF MILK, FAT AND TEMPERATURE

Date, Nov., 1899.	Time.	Pounds of milk.	Per cent of fat.	Pounds of fat.	Temperature.		
					8 hrs. before milking.	At time of milking.	Average.
16	5 A.M.	13.3	4.2	.559	101.4	101.6	101.50
	*4 P.M.	11.3	2.9	.328	102.0	103.2	102.60
17	5 A.M.	12.2	—	—	103.0	104.0	103.50
	4 P.M.	7.2	4.1	.295	105.0	101.6	103.30
18	5 A.M.	14.0	4.6	.644	101.5	101.4	101.45
	4 P.M.	13.2	3.5	.462	101.2	101.8	101.50
19	5 A.M.	13.2	4.2	.554	102.0	102.0	102 00
	4 P.M.	10.6	3.2	.339	102.0	101.6	101.80
20	5 A.M.	12.8	4.4	.563	103.2	101.8	102.50
	4 P.M.	12.7	3.7	.470	101.7	102.0	101.85
21	5 A.M.	15.7	4.0	.628	102.0	101.5	101.75
	4 P.M.	13.3	3.2	.426	101.6	101.5	101.55
22	5 A.M.	13.5	4.2	.567	101.4	101.6	101.50
	†4 P.M.	8.8	2.8	.246	101.4	102.2	101.80
23	5 A.M.	7.7	5.6	.431	102.8	101.7	102.25
	4 P.M.	8.8	4.4	.387	101.6	101.3	101.45
24	5 A.M.	12.5	3.8	.475	101.2	101.4	101.30
	4 P.M.	12.1	3.4	.411	102.0	103.0	102.50
25	5 A.M.	12.1	3.4	.411	102.5	101.8	102.15
	4 P.M.	10.7	3.1	.332	102.2	102.2	102.20
26	5 A.M.	15.8	3.0	.474	102.0	101.8	101.90
	4 P.M.	12.0	3.3	.396	102.0	102.0	102.00
27	5 A.M.	15.3	3.1	.474	101.5	101.6	101.55
	4 P.M.	12.7	3.2	.406	101.8	102.0	101.90
28	5 A.M.	14.3	3.4	.486	101.6	101.6	101.60
	4 P.M.	11.7	3.0	.351	102 8	102.0	102.40

* One quarter of udder feverish.
† Spayed at 2 P.M.

III. Temperature taken every four hours
GLISTA DE KOL
INDIVIDUAL RECORDS OF MILK, FAT AND TEMPERATURE

Date, Nov. 1899.	Time.	Pounds of milk.	Per cent of fat.	Pounds of fat.	Temperature.			
					8 hrs. before milking.	4 hrs. before milking.	At time of milking.	Average.
6–7	4 P.M.	11.4	3.1	.353	101.4	100.9	101.3	101.20
	5 A.M.	14.0	3.2	.448	101.2	101.0	101.8	101.33
7–8	4 P.M.	13.1	3.1	.406	101.6	101.0	101.6	101.40
	5 A.M.	12.8	3.2	.410	101.1	101.2	101.8	101.37
8–9	4 P.M.	10.9	3.1	.338	102.0	101.4	102.0	101.80
	5 A.M.	14.1	3.0	.423	101.6	101.6	101.3	101.50
9–10	4 P.M.	11.2	3.3	.370	101.6	101.2	101.1	101.30
	5 A.M.	13.3	3.2	.426	101.7	101.3	101.4	101.47
10–11	4 P.M.	11.0	3.2	.352	101.6	101.0	101.2	101.27
	5 A.M.	12.7	3.1	.394	101.5	101.7	101.5	101.57

TABLE V—(*Continued*)
III. Temperature taken every four hours
KATE (3)
INDIVIDUAL RECORDS OF MILK, FAT AND TEMPERATURE

Date, Nov. 1899.	Time.	Pounds of milk.	Per cent of fat.	Pounds of fat.	Temperature.			
					8 hrs. before milking.	4 hrs. before milking.	At time of milking.	Average.
6–7	4 P.M.	11.3	3.9	.441	101.8	100.5	101.8	101.37
	5 A.M.	12.0	4.1	.492	101.1	101.2	101.4	101.23
7–8	4 P.M.	10.2	3.6	.367	102.0	101.0	101.4	101.47
	5 A.M.	13.0	3.8	.494	101.0	101.1	101.5	101.20
8–9	4 P.M.	10.0	2.9	.290	101.7	101.2	101.7	101.53
	5 A.M.	13.0	2.8	.364	101.0	101.1	101.5	101.20
9–10	4 P.M.	10.8	3.2	.346	102.0	101.3	101.5	101.60
	5 A.M.	13.3	3.8	.505	100.8	101.0	101.4	101.07
10–11	4 P.M.	9.5	2.4	.228	101.5	101.5	101.6	101.53
	5 A.M.	12.2	3.6	.439	101.0	101.2	101.4	101.20
11–12	4 P.M.	9.0	2.7	.243	101.4	—–	101.5	101.45
	5 A.M.	12.8	3.3	.422	101.0	—–	101.2	101.10

III. Temperature taken every four hours
VALERIE EXILE
INDIVIDUAL RECORDS OF MILK, FAT AND TEMPERATURES

Date, Nov. 1899.	Time.	Pounds of milk.	Per cent of fat.	Pounds of fat.	Temperature.			
					8 hrs. before milking.	4 hrs. before milking.	At time of milking.	Average.
6–7	4 P.M.	4.5	5.1	.230	102.4	101.9	102.0	102.10
	5 A.M.	.5.2	4.8	.250	101.9	101.7	101.8	101.80
7–8	4 P.M.	4.5	4.2	.189	101.9	101.4	101.7	101.68
	5 A.M.	6.4	4.5	.288	101.5	101.3	101.9	101.57
8–9	4 P.M.	4.7	4.2	.297	102.0	101.4	102.0	101.80
	5 A.M.	6.0	3.9	.234	101.6	101.8	101.8	101.73
9–10	4 P.M.	5.0	4.8	.240	101.7	101.5	101.5	101.57
	5 A.M.	6.0	4.6	.276	101.7	101.7	101.8	101.73
10–11	4 P.M.	4.3	4.6	.298	102.0	101.8	101.9	101.90
	5 A.M.	5.7	4.3	.245	101.8	101.3	101.8	101.63
11–12	4 P.M.	4.5	4.5	.203	101.8	—–	101.9	101.85
	5 A.M.	6.0	4.2	.252	101.6	—–	102.0	101.80
VALERIE ST. LAMBERT								
6–7	4 P.M.	9.2	5.0	.460	101.2	101.0	101.6	101.27
	5 A.M.	10.0	4.4	.440	101.0	101.0	101.0	101.0
7–8	4 P.M.	10.5	4.9	.515	101.5	100.8	101.5	101.27
	5 A.M.	10.0	4.7	.470	101.3	100.8	101.4	101.17
8–9	4 P.M.	9.5	4.9	.466	101.2	100.8	101.2	101.07
	5 A.M.	11.0	4.6	.506	101.2	101.0	101.4	101.20
9–10	4 P.M.	11.0	5.0	.550	101.0	101.0	101.4	101.13
	5 A.M.	10.5	4.7	.494	101.2	100.8	101.5	101.17
10–11	4 P.M.	9.5	4.6	.437	100.7	100.7	101.3	100.90
	5 A.M.	11.0	4.8	.528	100.8	101.3	101.5	101.20
11–12	4 P.M.	9.5	4.5	.428	101.5	—–	101.8	101.65
	5 A.M.	10.5	4.6	.483	101.0	—–	101.5	101.25

I. INFLUENCE OF OESTRUM

Referring at the beginning to the influence of oestrum upon milk secretion the records show a variety of testimony. They seem to demonstrate that whatever effect the oestrum may have, its influence upon the yield and quality of milk may not be shown only upon the same day that the cow is observed to be in the heat period. This influence may manifest itself so far as the milk is concerned a day or two before or after oestrum. A few instances will serve to indicate this. The milk of Emma (1) contained a higher percentage of fat on the two days preceding oestrum than either on this particular day or any other day of the period of record. And since the amount of milk given on the two days was likewise slightly higher than the average daily yield, the total amount of butter-fat for each day was correspondingly higher than usual. The temperature of the cow remained uniform. On the day preceding oestrum Julia (3) gave more milk than on any other one of the eleven days of record. The percentage of fat in this day's milk was slightly higher than usual especially for the evening milking. She showed her ordinary body temperature upon this day but her temperature was higher than usual upon the day of oestrum.

Taken as a whole the influence of oestrum upon the yield of milk is slight. About two-thirds of the records show no perceptible change that can be attributed directly to this influence. The other third show for the most part a decrease in the yield of milk but the variation is slight. The influence upon the percentage of fat and the total yield of fat is more marked. From one-third to one-half of the cows show an increase in this respect ; one or two show a decrease, while the remainder show little or no change. The instance of the most remarkable variation is that of Julia (1). On the morning of the oestrum day she gave about four pounds less milk than usual which contained 1.55 per cent fat. At the evening milking she gave four or five pounds of milk more than usual which contained 4.75 per cent fat. The result was that the total butter-fat produced was .250 pounds in the morning and 1.378 pounds in the evening. On the second day following oestrum she had returned to her normal flow and quality of milk. Her temperature was higher than usual upon the oestrum day but no higher than at the two evening milkings four and five days following.

The temperature of the cows shows a noticeable rise in about two-thirds of the records, on or near the day of oestrum. In only one case, that of Ruby (2) was the body temperature lower than the average on this particular day. In one-third of the instances there appears no perceptible variation in temperature at the oestrum period. The most remarkable rise in temperature was that of Ruth. On the morning of the second day preceding oestrum her temperature was 105.4 and remained above 102 until the evening of the first day following oestrum.

A general survey of the records leads to the conclusion that the period of oestrum is accompanied by little variation in the flow of milk ; by a rise in butter fat percentage in about one-half the cases and no change in the other half ; by a variation in the total fat secreted corresponding to the variation in per cent of fat ; and usually by a rise in temperature. It cannot be held that the individuality of the cow is a governing factor in this connection, for in the three records taken from Julia she shows a larger degree of variation than is found between the records of different cows. A glance at the charts on subsequent pages will clearly display this point.

II.   INFLUENCE OF SPAYING

The records of the two cows given under this head show only the immediate effect of spaying upon the secretion of milk and they well illustrate how differently two animals may be effected by the same operation. Both cows were spayed at two o'clock in the afternoon. When milked at four o'clock Emma gave within a pound or two of her usual evening flow. The percentage of fat was one-half of one per cent higher than usual for the evening milking. Her flow of milk on the following day was 18.3 pounds as against 38.3 pounds for the day preceding the operation. The milk of the following day contained 4.9 and 3.8 per cent of fat for the morning and evening respectively, as against a per cent ranging from 2.5 to 3.0 before spaying. Her milk returned to its normal quality on the third day after the operation but the former quantity was not yet reached when the record ceased on the sixth day. Her temperature showed a perceptible rise immediately after she 'was spayed and became normal on the second day following.

Ruth gave about four pounds less milk than usual at the milking immediately following the operation and the per cent of fat therein was 2.8, which was four-tenths less than the usual evening test for her milk. Her yield of milk was still less on the following day after which it gained rapidly and reached the normal flow on the fourth day following spaying. Her milk contained a much higher per cent of fat than usual on the day after the operation and then declined gradually until it reached a point lower than before spaying. It should be said in this connection that the milk of this cow was not normal, either in quantity or quality at the beginning of the record, owing probably to the feverish condition of the udder. The quality of her milk as shown at the close of the record period corresponds closely with the quality of her milk in previous years. In temperature, Ruth showed a slight rise for twenty-four hours after spaying, but not to so high a degree as was reached on several instances both before and after the operation.

III. RELATION OF TEMPERATURE TO SECRETION OF MILK FAT

The problem to solve in this connection is whether or not the variations in the percentage of fat occur simultaneously with and in the same direction as the temperature of the animal and also whether or not the total butter-fat secreted at each milking varies in unison with the variations in temperature. A study of the figures in Table V will show that there is no regularity in either of these respects. On some days the lower temperature occurs with the lower percentage of fat for the day's milking and again with the higher percentage. The same feature obtains as regards the relation of the temperature with the total butter fat secreted. In order to render the data more easily interpreted there is arranged in Table VI the number of days on which the lower per cent of fat and lesser pounds of fat for each day occur with the lower and higher temperature for the day. That is, taking each day separately, the table shows the number of times that the lower per cent of fat and lesser pounds of fat fall simultaneously with the lower and higher temperature as recorded for the day for each cow. It is unnecessary to tabulate the figures for the higher percentages and larger amounts of butter fat since they are readily obtained by taking the differences between the figures given in the table and the total number of days. In making up the table no account has been taken of the days on which the temperatures, percentages of fat or pounds of fat were the same for both morning and evening milking.

TABLE VI

	Total number days.	Number of days on which the lower per cent of fat occurred with the		Total number days.	Number of days on which the lesser pounds of fat occurred with the	
		Lower temperature.	Higher temperature.		Lower temperature.	Higher temperature.
Ada	6	2	4	7	2	5
Belle	7	6	1	7	6	1
Belva 2d.........	7	4	3	9	5	4
Emma (1)........	8	5	3	9	3	6
Emma (2)	10	6	4	10	3	7
Floss	9	5	4	9	3	6
Ida	6	3	3	8	4	4
Julia (1)	10	9	1	10	4	6
Julia (2)..........	10	7	3	10	7	3
Julia (3)	9	8	1	9	3	6
Kate (1)	7	7	—	8	—	8
Kate (2)	7	6	1	8	1	7
Mabel 2d (1)......	9	5	4	9	4	5
Mabel 2d (2)......	11	4	7	11	3	8
Ruby (1)..........	7	3	4	7	2	5
Ruby (2)..........	10	6	4	11	4	7
Ruth (1)..........	9	4	5	9	2	7
Emma (3)	13	9	4	13	5	8
Ruth (2)..........	11	4	7	11	2	9
Glista De Kol.....	5	3	2	5	4	1
Kate (3)	6	2	4	6	1	5
Valerie Exile......	6	4	2	6	5	1
Valerie St. Lambert	6	3	3	6	4	2
Total	189	115	74	198	80	118
Per cent of total.		60.8	39.2		40.4	59.6

A glance at the figures in the table shows that on 60.8 per cent of the days of record, the lower per cent of fat in the cow's milk for the day occurred with the lower temperature of the cow recorded for the day: and that on 39.2 per cent of the days, the lower per cent of fat occurred with the higher temperature of the cow. The reverse is true with the pounds of fat. On 40.4 per cent of the days, the smaller yield of fat for each day occurred with the lower temperature, and 59.6 per cent with the higher temperature of the cow. If the lower per cent of fat was always accompanied by the smaller yield of fat of the two milkings of the day we would not expect the result as found above : but since the total yield of fat depends quite as much upon the amount of milk as upon the percentage of fat contained therein, the result as shown in the table is not surprising.

While the general tendency of the individual cows was to possess the lower body temperature coincident with producing the milk lower in fat content still there are a few which showed a tendency in the opposite direction. Kate (1) and (2) produced milk in which the lower per cent of fat for the day fell uniformly with her lower temperature for the same days. But later (3) two-thirds of her lower daily per cents of fat fell with the higher body temperature. Her case is of interest likewise in that in (1) and (2) all but one of her lower daily pounds of fat occurred at the same time with her higher temperature for the day. This same rule holds true in her later record (3). Referring to Table VIII it will be noticed that Kate (1) and (2), on 16 out of 17 days, secreted a lower percentage of fat in her morning's than in her evening's milk. But the total fat produced was greater with the lower than with the higher percentages of fat. In (3) her record was reversed in both respects.

Inasmuch as the temperatures of four of the cows were taken at intervals of four hours and of two of the cows at milking time and eight hours previous thereto, it will be of interest to compare the records of the average temperature between milkings and of the temperature at milking time on the basis of the foregoing table. Such comparison is given in Table VII. The results show that the average temperature compares more closely with the figures in Table VI when considering the percentages of fat : and that the single temperature taken at milking time compares more closely with Table VI when considering the total pounds of fat. In no case is there a strong indication that a close relation can be traced either between the percentage of fat or total yield of fat and the temperature of the animal.

TABLE VII

COMPARISON BETWEEN RESULTS OF TAKING TEMPERATURE OF COW AT TIME OF MILKING ONLY, OR OF TAKING THE AVERAGE TEMPERATURE FOR THE DAY, WHEN CALCULATING THE NUMBER OF DAYS ON WHICH THE LOWER PER CENT OF FAT AND POUNDS OF FAT OCCURRED WITH THE LOWER OR HIGHER TEMPERATURE

	Temperature taken at milking only.			Temperature, average from two or three observations.		
	Total number days.	Number of days on which lower per cent of fat occurred with the		Total number days.	Number of days on which lower per cent of fat occurred with the	
		Lower temperature.	Higher temperature.		Lower temperature.	Higher temperature.
Emma (3)..........	13	9	4	13	10	3
Ruth (2)...........	11	4	7	12	6	6
Glista de Kol......	5	3	2	5	2	3
Kate (3)......	6	1	5	6	2	4
Valerie Exile	6	4	2	6	4	2
Valerie St. Lambert	6	3	3	6	3	3
Total.......	47	24	23	48	27	21
Per cent of total..		51	49		56.3	43.7
Number of days on which the lesser pounds of fat occurred in relation to temperature as per column heading.						
Emma (3)..........	13	5	8	13	2	11
Ruth (2)..........	11	2	9	12	4	8
Glista De Kol......	5	4	1	5	2	3
Kate (3)...........	6	1	5	6	—	6
Valerie Exile	6	5	1	6	3	3
Valerie St. Lambert	6	4	2	6	4	2
Total.............	47	21	26	48	15	33
Per cent of total..		44.7	55.3		31.3	68.7

CHARTS

The following diagrams show the records of three of the cows as taken from Table V. The influence of oestrum on milk production is represented by the records of Emma and Julia, the former having had two, and the latter three record periods. The influence of spaying is represented by nine days each from the records of Emma and Ruth. The time of milking is indicated by the letters at the top of each chart, A and P meaning morning and evening, respectively. On the seven diagrams, each space counting vertically, represents two-tenths of one pound of milk, one-tenth of one per cent of fat, one one-hundredth of one pound of fat or one-tenth of one degree of temperature as the case may be. The day on which oestrum or spaying occurred is indicated by the heavy vertical line drawn through the chart midway between the points which are noted by A and P as the morning and evening milkings of that particular day.

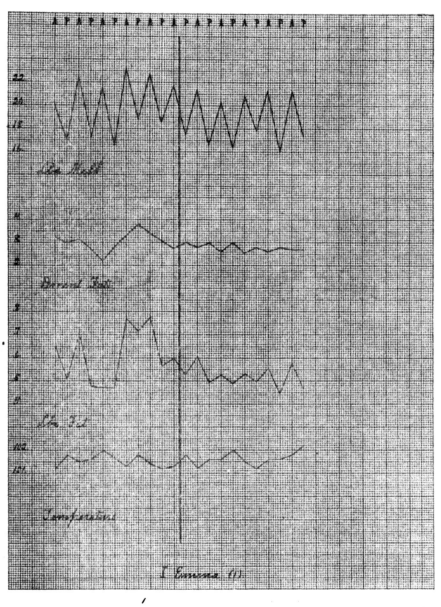

7 —Diagram showing influence of oestrum on milk production. The oestrum day is indicated by the heavy vertical line. A, morning. P, evening.

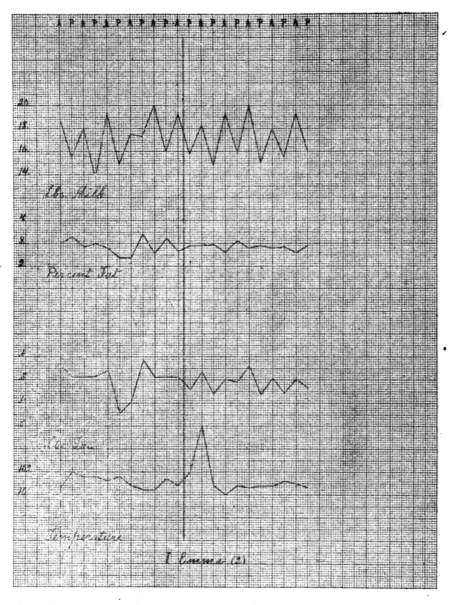

8.—*Diagram showing influence of oestrum on milk production. The oestrum day is indicated by the heavy vertical line. A, morning. P, evening.*

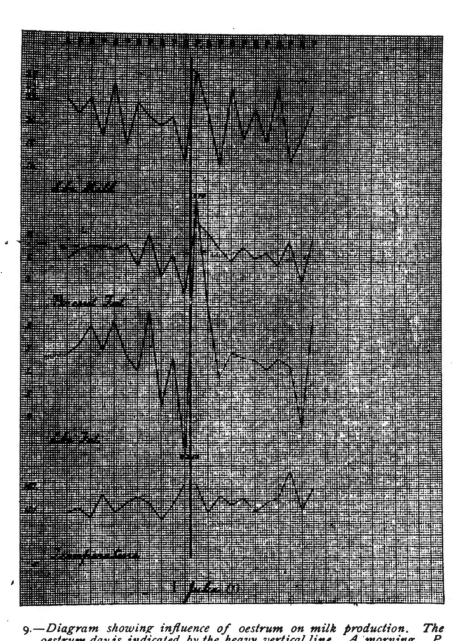

9.—*Diagram showing influence of oestrum on milk production. The oestrum day is indicated by the heavy vertical line. A, morning. P, evening.*

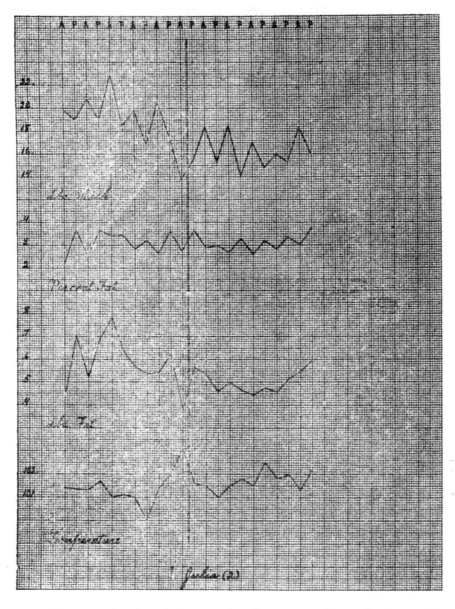

10.—*Diagram showing influence of oestrum on milk production. The oestrum day is indicated by the heavy vertical line. A, morning. P. evening.*

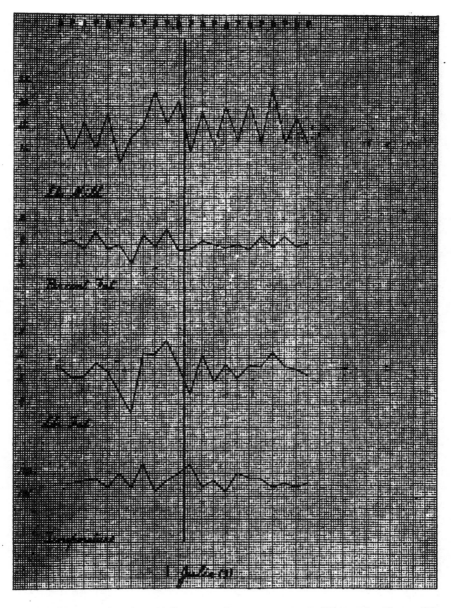

11.—*Diagram showing influence of oestrum on milk production. The oestrum day is indicated by the heavy vertical line. A, morning. P, evening.*

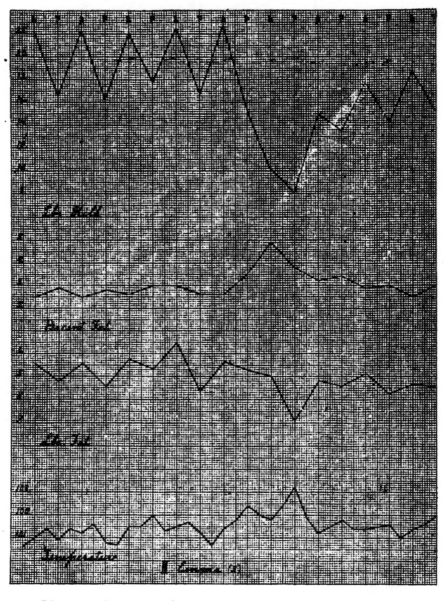

12.—*Diagram showing influence of spaying on milk production. The day of spaying is indicated by the heavy vertical line. A, morning. P, evening.*

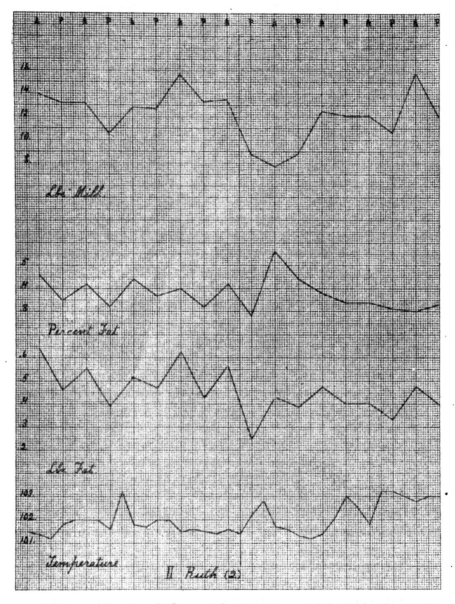

13.—*Diagram showing influence of spaying on milk production. The day of spaying is indicated by the heavy vertical line.   A, morning. P, evening.*

THE RELATION OF PERCENTAGE OF FAT TO TOTAL POUNDS OF FAT

A more important deduction than any yet made from Table V, is that in the relation between the percentage of fat and the total fat secreted at each milking. A large amount of experimenting has been done and a great deal of space devoted to discussion, to determine the cause of the variation in the quality of the milk of individual cows, but very little study has been devoted to the actual quantity of butter-fat secreted along with the varying percentages. It is not enough to know that a morning's milk contains one per cent less of fat than the night's milk. The question should be : is there as much butter-fat secreted in that morning's milk or the milking containing the lower percentage of fat as in the following milking of higher quality? So far as the physiology of milk secretion is concerned it seems to be of the highest importance to know if a cow will elaborate as much butter-fat during the night as during the day, regardless of the percentage of fat content.

The only reference to this question in Experiment Station literature that has come to the writer's notice is by Linfield.* The data which he gives however is based upon weekly composite samples of the morning and evening milkings separately. The period between evening and morning milking was thirteen to fourteen hours and between morning and evening milking, ten to eleven hours. Since the morning composite sample always tested higher than the evening sample and since the greater yield of milk was invariably given in the morning, the assumption was that the per cent of fat in each cow's milk was higher in the evening than in the morning. This was quite probably not true, since the higher percentage of fat does not always occur with the smaller yield of milk, as has been shown in these pages. Of the ten cows whose records were examined, Linfield says, " that five of them gave the most butter-fat when they gave the least milk," *i. e.* the evening milk which was higher in fat content than the morning milk.

---

* Utah Experiment Station Bulletin No. 68 p. 223.

The data which are herein compiled show, in Table VIII, the number of days on which the lower percentage of fat occurred with the smaller yield of milk and with the larger yield of milk ; and the number of days on which the lower percentage of fat occurred at the evening and at the morning milking. Table IX shows the number of days on which the lower percentage of fat for each day occurred simultaneously with the smaller yield of fat and the number of days with the larger yield of fat. This table also shows the total pounds of butter-fat which were secreted with the lower and higher percentages of fat respectively on each day of the record. In making up Table VIII no account has been taken of the days on which the percentage of fat or pounds of milk were the same at both morning and evening. In like manner, for Table IX those days were not included whereon the percentages of fat or pounds of fat were the same at each of the daily milkings.

It may be argued that the cows whose records are given were under unusual conditions and that the data then secured may be warped. Even granting this, it must be said that all of the cows except two were in such condition as obtains in every cow's life and with the exception of three or four records nothing developed sufficiently abnormal to exclude the cows from a record of this kind. Julia (1), Ruth (2) and Kate (3) showed unusual variations as have been previously noted and their records might justly be excluded from those of the other cows. It will be borne in mind that all the records have been compiled from the weight of milk and test for butter-fat of each milking for each individual cow ; and that the lower or higher percentage of fat, larger or smaller yield of milk or of fat refers to the observations taken within each twenty-four hours. The tabulated data follow :

TABLE VIII

	Total number days.	Number of days on which the lower per cent of fat occurred with the		Total number days.	Number of days on which the lower per cent of fat occurred.	
		Smaller yield of milk.	Larger yield of milk.		At evening.	At morning.
Ada..............	6	3	3	7	5	2
Belle	9	1	8	10	1	9
Belva 2d..........	8	3	5	8	1	7
Emma (1)	10	3	7	10	3	7
Emma (2)	11	1	10	11	1	10
Floss	9	4	5	9	3	6
Ida...............	9	2	7	9	2	7
Julia (1)..........	11	4	7	11	1	10
Julia (2)..........	11	1	10	11	—	11
Julia (3)..........	11	2	9	11	1	10
Kate (1)..........	9	—	9	9	—	9
Kate (2)	8	1	7	8	1	7
Mabel 2d (1)......	9	3	6	9	2	7
Mabel 2d (2)......	11	4	7	11	4	7
Ruby (1)..........	10	2	8	11	4	7
Ruby (2)..........	10	2	8	10	2	8
Ruth (1)	11	4	7	11	5	6
Emma (3)	13	2	11	13	2	11
Ruth (2)..........	12	9	3	12	2	10
Glista De Kol	5	1	4	5	2	3
Kate (3)	6	5	1	6	5	1
Valerie Eixle......	6	1	5	6	1	5
Valerie St. Lambert	6	4	2	6	2	4
Total..........	211	62	149	214	50	164
Per cent of total.		29.4	70.6		23.4	76.6

TABLE IX

	Total number days.	Number of days on which the lower per cent of fat occurred with the		Pounds of butter fat secreted	
		Smaller yield of fat.	Larger yield of fat.	At higher per cent fat.	At lower per cent fat.
Ada	7	5	2	3.140	2.958
Belle	10	4	6	7.730	7.177
Belva 2d..........	8	7	1	5.574	4.825
Emma (1)..........	10	3	7	5.773	5.604
Emma (2)	11	4	7	5.392	5.463
Floss	9	5	4	6.004	5.649
Ida...............	9	3	6	2.608	2.773
Julia (1)...........	11	6	5	8.773	6.655
Julia (2)...........	11	7	4	6.263	5.704
Julia (3)...........	11	5	6	6.057	5 966
Kate (1)...........	9	1	8	3.092	3.247
Kate (2)...........	8	1	7	2.728	2.891
Mabel 2d (1)	9	5	4	4.034	3.724
Mabel 2d (2).......	11	6	5	4.689	4.352
Ruby (1)	11	5	6	7.810	7.711
Ruby (2)	10	4	6	6.292	6.617
Ruth (1)...........	11	9	2	6.908	6.399
Emma (3).........	13	3	10	6.331	6.598
Ruth (2)	12	10	2	6.120	4.700
Glista De Kol......	5	2	3	1.918	2.002
Kate (3)...........	5	1	6	2.642	1.989
Valerie Exile......	6	3	3	1.556	1.446
Valerie St. Lambert	5	1	6	3.002	2.775
Total..........	214	108	106	114.436	107.225
Per cent of total..		50.5	49.5	51.6	48.4

In 211 days of record the lower percentage of fat occurred with the smaller yield of milk 62 times, or 29.4 per cent, and with the larger yield of milk 149 times, or 70.6 per cent. In 214 days of record the lower percentage of fat for the day was found in the evening's milk 50 times or 23.4 per cent and in the morning's milk 164 times or 76.6 per cent of the whole number. In a like number of days the lower percentage of fat occurred with the smaller yield of fat 108 times or 50.5 per cent and with the larger yield of fat, 106 times or 49.5 per cent of the whole number. The total amount of butter-fat secreted by the fourteen cows in 214 days was 221.661 pounds of which 51.6 per cent was secreted in that one of the two portions of the day's milk which contained the higher percentage of fat, and 48.4 per cent was secreted in that portion containing the lower percentage of fat. If the records of Julia (1), Ruth (2) and Kate (3) are excluded the remaining figures show that 50.8 per cent of the total fat was secreted at the higher percentage and 49.2 per cent was secreted at the lower percentage of fat.

With the exception of the three records just named there was little variation between the amounts of fat secreted respectively at the higher and lower percentages of fat by the individual cows. Emma (2) and (3), Ida, Kate (1) and (2), Ruby (2) and Glista De Kol secreted more fat at the lower than at the higher percentage. All the other records show a reverse order as to the larger production of total butter-fat. The conclusion to be drawn from the data is that when there was a variation in the percentage of butter-fat between the morning's and evening's milking, that the amount of milk containing the lower percentage also contained very nearly as much total fat as the amount of milk containing the higher percentage of fat. It will be of interest and importance to carry this sort of investigation to a large number of animals and for longer periods. And it appears on the whole that experimenters have been paying too much attention to the actual variations in the quality of milk and not enough to the total fat secreted.

GENERAL SUMMARY

The influences which affect the secretion of milk may, for convenience in discussion, be classified as either transitory or permanent. By transitory is meant those influences which cause such changes in the quantity or quality of milk as continue for a more or less brief period and then the milk returns to its former normal amount and composition, regardless of whether or not the moulding influence be continued. Under this head may be classed heat, cold, fatigue, unusual or sudden changes in food and the like. By permanent influences are meant those whose effect is so fixed in the constitution of the animal that whatever change has taken place in the milk secreted will continue so long as the moulding influence be continued. Such influences as heredity, environment or food may be classed as permanent, but only and always upon the above named condition of the continuity of the cause of the change.

Reference has been made on page 33 to the effect of radical changes in food upon milk secretion and in that connection the matter of the proper length of experimental periods was discussed. A difference of opinion has arisen therein as to what effects may be considered transitory and what permanent. Hills* considers four or five weeks a sufficiently long period to secure a permanent effect. Lindsey † holds that a period of such length can not be counted upon to give permanent results, as is evidenced by the following quotation from the source named : "The fat increase was only temporary, the milk gradually returning (in four or five weeks) to its normal fat content."

But the root of the matter is not so much to fix the length of period for all experiments as it is to ascertain the actual effect of the food upon the animal. The proper length of any experimental period is dependent upon the character of the food and upon the manner in which the animal receives it. If the food cause any disturbance of digestion or assimilation, the animal will need a longer time to become accustomed thereto. And whether the animal does or does not become accustomed to the

---

* Vermont Station, Annual Reports, 1900, p. 417, 1901, p. 369.
† Massachusetts (Hatch) Station, Annual Report, 1901, p. 14.

food may determine the transitoriness or permanency of its effect.

Of the forty-nine experiments summarized in the earlier pages of this paper, the large majority of them report experimental periods of five weeks or less. And of those wherein was claimed to be found an increase in the quality of milk as the direct influence of the food, Kühn's experiment (page 26) is the only one reporting periods of more than five weeks. Kühn states that his experimental periods were from twenty-one to forty-seven days in length. Moreover, a glance at the tabulation on page 32, shows that the foods which seem most potent in increasing the quality of milk, viz.: fat in various forms and molasses mixtures are the foods most likely to cause internal disorders of the animal, outwardly noticeable or unnoticeable, and a consequent fluctuation in the percentage of butter-fat.

In the light of these facts, may it not rightly be doubted that any experiment has yet proven that a *permanent* increase in the quality of milk is possible as the direct result of food? May we not go so far as to hold that the most that any experiment, calculated to demonstrate the influence of food upon milk fat, has done is to show a transitory effect as the result of the changed feeding? It has been the fault of the investigator if he has not carried the experiment long enough to prove beyond doubt that the effect of the food might have been permanent rather than transitory.

But so long as the cow is sufficiently nourished, why should any food or combination of foods increase the proportion of butter-fat in milk? According to the latest investigations* "the fat of milk is a true product of secretion—a product of the life activity of the cells and not a product of their degeneration." And it seems just to believe that the epithelial cells of the udder are subject to similar physiological laws as other secretory cells of the body. In defining metabolism, Piersol† says that "the cell selects and assimilates from the surrounding food materials those substances adapted to the particular needs of its own nutrition and function, so changing and

---

*Disselhorst in Ztschr. Fleisch und Milch hyg., 8, No. 8, p. 146. Abs. in E. S. R. 10, p. 282.

† Histology p. 15.

incorporating into its substance the materials thus acquired that they become an integral part of the cell. By a still further exercise of this process, the assimilated materials are converted into new substances which may be retained within the cell or, as is frequently the case, given up as the various secretions of the body." According to Kühn* "the living protoplasm of the animal cell is not the same as the proteid on which it feeds. It is a much more complex substance, mobile and constantly changing, which receives into itself, and as a part of its unstable self, the nutrients of the food, whether nitrogenous or non-nitrogenous; and the further changes which take place and which build up the substances of the body, or produce its heat and force, are changes depending on the unstable and ever changing nature of the living molecule, and take place in the living substance itself. . .

. . . According to this view the formation of fat does not take place from proteids or from carbohydrates, or even from fats themselves present in the food, but from the living plasm which these go to nourish. Proteids or fats or carbohydrates may furnish the material to make fat, but only by themselves first ceasing to be proteid, fat or carbohydrate and becoming an integral part of the complex living substance from which the fat is afterwards split off." The protoplasm of each cell is, as it were, a law unto itself and any change made in the form or function of the animal must come through a variation in the cell nutrition and secretion.

The matter depends, then, upon the question as to what extent the secretion of milk fat is a part of the natural function of the epithelial cells. But since milk fat has been found to be a true secretory product it naturally follows that it is the function of the epithelial cells to secrete this fat. The salivary glands of the infant child do not secrete ptyalin. More or less food, rich or poor food has no effect upon the secretion except so far as the lack of food would impoverish and weaken the general system. The salivary glands begin to secrete ptyalin when the infant reaches the age that nature has provided for such secretion to begin. And "what nature has provided" consists of the sum of two factors, heredity and individuality.

* Landwirthschaftliche Versuchs-Stationen, 44 (1894) p. 257.

The animal cell, whether secretory or non-secretory is what it is in structure and function by reason of a long heredity made up of habit, nutrition and use. The capacity for producing milk and the composition of the milk produced is, therefore, governed by the heredity of the cow plus that indefinable quality called individuality, which may consist, however, more largely of heredity than any observer can fathom. The amount of milk that may be produced depends quite as largely upon the quantity and quality of the nourishment provided as upon any hereditary tendencies. There may be ever so rich an inheritance of cellular structure designed to elaborate milk, but if food for the cells be wanting they cannot perform their natural function to the full capacity.

Nothing contained herein is intended to be construed to contradict the belief expressed in previous pages that the natural tendency of a very succulent or watery diet is to produce milk containing a low percentage of solids and of a concentrated diet to produce milk containing a high percentage of solids. But causes such as these must be continued for generations to become fixed to such a degree that they may be looked upon as permanent race characteristics. Such natural tendencies, however, give the breeder the clew of how to improve the milking qualities of his cattle. Abundance of proper food is necessary that the animal may be sufficiently nourished in all of its parts and the flow of milk kept thereby to the maximum capacity of the animal. The tendencies are then in the right direction and variations are likely to occur in one generation after another, whereby an improvement is quite as apt to be noted in the quality as in the quantity of milk from succeeding offspring, which variation may be accentuated by the practice of a wise selection. The remarks made in this summary are rather intended to point to the probability that no experiment has yet proven that an increase in the percentage of fat in milk is possible as a result solely of feeding, and to indicate a few reasons why the experiments have failed to prove this.

CONCLUSIONS FROM EXPERIMENTS

For two terms of twenty-two weeks, nine cows were fed in lots of three each on different rations, the nutritive ratios of which were about 1:4, 1:6, and 1:9 respectively.   During this time the percentage of fat in the milk of each lot increased slightly and gradually without regard to the kind of ration.   For continuous feeding, the medium ration appeared to give better results as to yield of milk than either the narrow or wide rations.

When the food of six cows was changed from the usual ration to one containing from four to seven pounds of palm nut meal and then, after six weeks, to the usual ration again, there were variations in the fat content of the milk, but no more nor greater than when the food of the cows was unchanged.

The period of oestrum as observed with eleven cows was accompanied by little variation in the flow of milk ; by a rise in butter-fat percentage in about one-half the cases and little or no change in the other half ; by a variation in the total fat secreted corresponding to the variation in the percentage of fat : and usually by a rise in temperature.   Each cow returned to her normal milk secretion as soon as the oestrum period had passed.

Two cows that were spayed · showed a large decrease in milk flow, a wide fluctuation in the percentage of fat and a slight rise in temperature immediately following the operation.   Both cows recovered their normal condition and flow of milk within a few days.

The results of a study extending over a period of 214 days of record with fourteen different cows indicate that there is no intimate relation between the temperature of the cow and either the percentage of fat or the total yield of fat.   There appears to be no difference in this respect whether the temperature be taken only at milking time or at more frequent intervals.

In 214 days of record the lower per cent of fat for each day occurred 62 times with the smaller yield of milk and 149 times with the larger yield of milk ; 50 times at the evening milking and 164 times at the morning milking ; and 108 times with the smaller yield of fat and 106 times with the larger yield of fat.

In 214 days of record with fourteen different cows and comparing the morning's with the night's milking on each day, 51.6 per cent of the total butter-fat produced was secreted at the milkings containing the higher percentage of fat, and 48.4 per cent of the total butter-fat was secreted at the milkings containing the lower percentage of fat.

BIBLIOGRAPHY

Literature of Experimentation Touching upon the Production of Milk

I. AGRICULTURAL EXPERIMENT STATION BULLETINS.

Alabama, 114.—Duggar and Clark. Feeding Experiments with Dairy Cows.

Arizona, 39.—True. Dairy Herd Records.

California, 132.—Jaffa and Anderson. Feeding Farm Animals : Sugar Beet Pulp.

Colorado, 20.—Quick. Influence of Food upon the Pure Fat Present in Milk.

Connecticut (Storrs), 13.—Woods and Phelps. Rations Fed to Milch Cows in Connecticut.

20.—Beach. A Study of Dairy Cows.

Delaware, 46.—Neale. Dairy Value of Pea Vine Silage compared with that of June Pasture.

Georgia, 49.—Wing. Feeding Experiments.

Illinois, 17.- Farrington. Daily Variations in Milk Production.

24.—Farrington. Variations in Milk.

33.—Morrow. Certified Tests of Dairy Cows.

51.—Davenport and Fraser. Variations in Milk and Milk Production.

Indiana, 24.—Wulff. Experiments in Milk Production.

47.—Plumb. Does it Pay to Shelter Milch Cows in Winter?

Iowa, 13.—Wilson, *et al.* Experiment in Feeding for Milk.

14.—Wilson, *et al.* Effect of Feed on Quality of Milk.

25.—Wilson, *et al.* Feeding Winter Dairy Cows.

32.—Wilson, *et al.* Feeding Dairy Cows and Feeding Cottonseed Meal to Dairy Cows.

36.—Wilson and McKay. Effect of Period of Lactation on Milk and Quality of Butter.

Kansas, 81.—Cottrell. Feed and Care of the Dairy Cow.

Maryland, 69.—Doane. The Influence of Feed and Care on the Individuality of Cows.

Massachusetts (State), 10.—Goessmann. Feeding Experiments with Corn Ensilage.

12.—Goessmann. Notes on Feeding Experiment with Gluten Meal as Constituent of Daily Diet of Milch Cows.

32.—Goessmann. Experiments to Ascertain Cost of Food for Production of Milk.

15, 22, 27, 35, 38, 41, 42.—Goessmann. Feeding Experiments with Milch Cows.

Massachusetts (Hatch), 39.—Lindsey. Economic Feeding of Milch Cows.

Michigan, 41.—Johnson. Warming Water for Dairy Cows.

149.—Smith. Feeding Dairy Cows.

166.—Smith. A Grade Dairy Herd.

193.—Smith. Feeding Beet Pulp to Dairy Cows.

Minnesota, 4.—Porter. Comparative Value of Cold and Warm Water in the Production of Milk.

35.—Haecker. Dairy Herd Record for 1893.

67.—Haecker. Investigations in Milk Production : Feeding Dairy Cows.

71.—Haecker and Major. Investigations in Milk Production.

Mississippi, 13, 15, 21.—Lloyd. Feeding for Milk and Butter.

60.—Moore. Feeding Cottonseed, Cottonseed Meal and Corn to Dairy Cows : Influence of Feed on Quality of Milk and Butter.

70.—Moore. Feeding Dairy Cows.

Nebraska, 30.—Ingersol and Duncanson. Influence of Changes of Food and Temperature on Quantity and Quality of Milk.

New Hampshire, 2, 8.—Whitcher. Feeding Experiments.

9, 13.—Whitcher. Effect of Food upon milk.

18.—Wood. Effect of Food upon Milk.

20.—Wood. Effect of Food upon Milk : Feeding with Fats.

New Jersey, 10.—Cook. Rational System of Feeding Milch Cows.

137.—Lane. The Yield, Composition and Cost of Milk : Experiments with Different Rations.

148.—Voorhees· and Lane. Alfalfa Protein vs. Purchased Protein in Rations for Dairy Cows.

New York (State) *Old Series*, 33.—Sturtevant. Influence of Food on Milk.

34, 35, 36.—Sturtevant. Feeding of Cows.

84.—Sturtevant. Silage for Cows.

104.—Sturtevant. Feeding for Milk.

106, 110, 114.—Sturtevant. Influence of Acid and Putrefactive Food upon Cows and their Milk.

New Series, 80.—Wheeler. Alfalfa Forage for Milch Cows.

97.—Wheeler. Corn Silage for Milch Cows.

105.—VanSlyke. Effects of Drought on Milk Production.

132.—Jordan and Jenter. The Source of Milk-Fat.

197.—Jordan, Jenter and Fuller. The Food Source of Milk-Fat.

210.—Wheeler. The Immediate Effect upon Milk Production of Changes in the Ration.

New York (Cornell University), 22, 36.—Roberts and Wing. Effect of Grain Ration for Cows with Pasturage and with Green Fodder.

52.—Wing. Cost of Milk Production : Variation in Individual Cows.

92.—Wing. Effect of Feeding Fat to Cows.

152.—Wing and Anderson. Studies in Milk Secretion : Drawn from Officially Authenticated Tests of Holstein-Friesian Cows.

169.—Wing and Anderson. Studies in Milk Secretion : Record of University Herd 1891–1898.

173.—Anderson. The Relation of Food to Milk Fat.

II. AGRICULTURAL EXPERIMENT STATION ANNUAL REPORTS.

necticut, 1893, p. 69; 1894, p. 26; 1895, p. 41. Atwater and Phelps. 1896, p. 53; 1897, p. 17. Phelps. 1900, p. 130.

Kansas.—Cottrell. The Milk and Butter Product as Influenced by Feeding, 1888, p. 69.

Maine.—Tests of Dairy Cows, 1890, p. 17.

Jordan. The Influence of Widely Differing Rations upon the Quantity and Quality of Milk, 1893, p. 73.

Jordan. Feeding Experiments with Milch Cows: Large or Small Hay Ration, 1894, p. 44.

Bartlett. Wheat Meal vs. Corn Meal: Ensilage of Mature Corn, Sunflower Heads and Peas, 1895, p. 24.

Bartlett. Gluten Meal vs. Cottonseed Meal; Ground Oats vs. Wheat Bran: Silage vs. Grain: Nutriotone for Milk Production, 1896, p. 37.

Bartlett. The Effect of Feeding Fat on the Fat Content of the Milk, 1898, p. 114.

Massachusetts (State).—A series of feeding experiments with milch cows extending over several years.

Goessmann. Corn Ensilage: Corn Ensilage with Gluten Meal, 1884, pp. 26, 42.

Various Grains and Coarse Fodders, 1885, p. 10.

Corn Stover vs. English Hay: Corn Ensilage vs. Beet Roots, 1886, p. 11.

English Hay, Corn Fodder, Fodder Corn, Ensilage, Roots and Soiling Crops, 1887, p. 11.

Various Grains and Dry and Green Fodders, 1888, p. 11; 1889, p. 12.

Old Process vs. New Process Linseed Meal: Various Green Fodders, 1890, p. 12.

Old Process Linseed Meal vs. Chicago Gluten Meal: Chicago Gluten vs. Cottonseed Meal: Various Green Fodders, 1891, p. 14.

Dent Corn vs. Sweet Corn: Corn Meal vs. Chicago Maize Feed: Various Green Fodders, 1892, p. 14.

Lindsey. Various Grains and Dry and Green Coarse Fodders, 1893, p.12.

Comparative Valve of Different Coarse Fodders: Effect of Food upon the Cost and Quality of Milk, 1894, p. 32.

Massachusetts (Hatch).—Lindsey, *et al.* Chicago Gluten Meal vs. King Gluten Meal and vs. Atlas Meal, 1895 pp. 62, 65.

The Effect of Narrow and Wide Rations on the Quantity and Cost of Milk and Butter and on the Composition of Milk, 1896, p. 100.

Cottonseed Feed as a Hay Substitute for Milch Cows, 1897, p. 79.

Effect of Feed on the Composition of Milk, 1900, p. 14.

Michigan.—Johnson. Warming Water for Dairy Cows, 1888, p. 139. Same as Bulletin No. 41.

Johnson. Experiments with Corn Ensilage vs. Dry Corn Fodder, 1889, p. 205.

Smith. Feeding Dairy Cows, 1898, p. 250. Same as Bulletin No. 149.

New Jersey.—Lane. The Feeding Value of Ear Corn Compared with Corn and Cob Meal, 1898, p. 211.

Influence of Widely Differing Rations upon the Yield of Milk and Fat and upon the Composition of Milk, 1899, p. 202.

Experiments with Good and Poor Rations, 1899, p. 216.

Influence of Wide vs. Balanced Rations upon the Yield of Milk and Fat and upon the Composition of Milk, 1900, p. 266.

Lipman. The Yield and Composition of Milk Obtained when the Intervals between Milkings are Unequal and when they are Equal 1899, p. 220.

New York (State).—Sturtevant. Glucose or Starch Waste as Cattle Food, 1885, p. 16. Effect of Food upon Milk, 1887, p. 15.

Ladd. Influence of Food upon Milk and Butter, 1888, p. 284. Relative Feeding Value of Some Grain Rations, 1889, p. 198.

Collier. Effect of Various Foods upon Milk, 1890, p. 7.

The Source of Fat in Milk, 1891, p. 124.

Relation of Food to Milk, 1892, p. 143.

Relation of Fat in Food to Fat in Milk, 1894, p. 114.

Jordan and Jenter. The Source of Milk Fat, 1897, p. 491. Same as Bulletin No. 132.

Vermont.—A series of feeding experiments with milch cows extending over several years, with especial reference to quantity and quality of milk produced.

Hills. Test of Various Coarse Fodders and Pasturage, 1889, p. 51.

Effect of Heavy Grain Feeding : Some Coarse Fodders : and Change from Barn to Pasture, 1890, pp. 65-107.

Effect of Weather : Change from Barn to Pasture : and Change of Quarters : Silage vs. Corn Fodder, 1891, pp. 59-118.

Effect of Weather : Change from Barn to Pasture : and Various Grains and Coarse Fodders. Variations in Quantity and Quality of Milk from various Causes, 1892, pp. 89-197.

Effect of Weather and Change from Barn to Pasture. Feeding Bone Meal and Various Ensilages, 1893, pp. 70-118.

Effect of Fatigue. Feeding Robertson Mixture, Corn Ensilage and Beets, 1894, pp. 142-192.

Feeding Corn Ensilage, Beets, Carrots and Various Concentrates. Variations in Milk due to Various Causes, 1895, pp. 157-236.

Feeding Trials with Silage and Potatoes : Studies in Methods of Experimental Feeding Trials, 1896-7, pp. 134-220.

Effect of Fatigue : Feeding Tests and their Methods, 1897-8, pp. 310-400 : 1898-9, pp. 252-309 : 1899-1900, pp. 391-46c.

Effect of Feeding Germ-oil Meal : Addition of Excessive Amounts of Single Nutrients : A Comparison of Feeding Trial Methods, 1900-1901, pp. 314-375.

Wisconsin.—Henry. Corn Stalks vs. Mixed Hay and Clover Hay, 1884, p. 11.

Armsby. Value of Cottonseed Meal and Malt Sprouts, 1884, p. 78.

Henry. Cut vs. Uncut Corn Stalks : Soiling vs. Pasturage, 1885, pp. 9, 19.

Armsby. New Process Oil Meal vs. Corn Meal, 1885, p, 97.

Henry. Ensilage vs. Fodder Corn : Cut vs. Uncut Corn Fodder, 1886, pp. 25, 34.

Armsby. Bran vs. Corn Meal : Bran vs. Oil Meal : Influence of Nutritive Ratio upon Milk Products, 1886, pp. 115, 130, 147.

Henry. Ensilage vs. Dry Fodder Corn, 1887-8, p. 5.

Woll. Ensilage vs. Fodder Corn, 1887-8, p. 28.

Woll. Corn Ensilage vs. Dry Fodder : Fodder Corn vs. Corn Ensilage as Exclusive Feeds, 1889, pp. 71, 106.

Short. Ensilage vs. Fodder Corn, 1889, p. 130.

King. Comparative Value of Warm and Cold Water, 1889, p. 146 ; 1890, p. 163.

Woll. Ground Oats vs. Bran : Corn Ensilage vs. Dry Fodder Corn, 1890, pp. 65, 80.

Woll. Relative Value of Corn Silage and Field Cured Fodder Corn, 1891, p. 49.

King. Influence of Imperfect Ventilation, 1891, p. 61.

Henry, Woll and Short. Feeding and Digestion Experiments with Milch Cows, 1882-1893 ; 1893, pp. 64-94.

Woll. Comparative Value of Linseed Meal, Corn Meal and Wheat Bran, 1894, p. 113.

Woll and Carlyle. Economy of Heavy Grain Feeding, 1899, p. 52 ; 1900, p. 37.

Carlyle. Effect on Dairy Cows of Changing Milkers, 1899, p. 89.

Carlyle. Record of University Dairy Herd, 1899, p. 68 ; 1900 p. 314.

III a. ONTARIO AGRICULTURAL COLLEGE AND EXPERIMENT FARM.

Annual Reports

Influence of Food on Dairy Products, 1883, p. 66.

Feeding Ensilage and Turnips, 1885, p. 114.

Effect of Extra Summer Fodder on the Quantity and Quality of Milk, 1887, p. 137.

The Effect of Food on the Quality and Quantity of Milk, 1891,p. 154.

Effect of Food on Milk and Butter, 1892, p. 204.

Effect of Food on Fat in Milk ; Feeding Slop and Wheat, 1893, pp. 148-151.

Feeding Silage : Effect of Feeding Turnips, 1897, pp. 59, 62.

Green Oats and Peas and Oats and Tares as Soiling Crops for Milch Cows ; Sugar Beets vs. Mangels, 1898, pp. 78, 80.

Mangels vs. Turnips : Mangels vs. Sugar Beets, 1899, pp. 71, 76.

Apples, Apple Pomace, Rape and Turnips for Dairy Cows,1900,VI. p.41.

III b. TRANSACTIONS OF THE HIGHLAND AND AGRICULTURAL SOCIETY, SCOTLAND.

Spier. The Effects of Food upon Milk and Butter, 1894, p. 83 ; 1896, p. 269 ; 1897, p. 296.

IV. SOME FOREIGN EXPERIMENTATION ON MILK PRODUCTION.

Landwirtschaftlichen   Versuchs-Stationen.—Lehmann. Zusammensetzung der Milch einer perlsüchtigen Kuh, V. 3, p. 195.

Müller. Die Veränderungen in der Zusammensetzung der Milch, welche von der Zeit des Kalbens abhängen, V. 6, p. 376.

Fleischmann und Vieth. Beodachtungen über die Milchsecretion und die Fettgehalt der Milch an einer grösseren Kuhheerde, 24 (1880) p. 81.

Siewert   Ueber den Einfluss der ungeshälten Baumwollsamenkuchen auf die Milchproduction, 30 (1884) p. 145.

Gebek. Einwirkung des Kokosnusskuchen und Kokosnussmehl auf die Mastung, Ertrag und Beschaffenheit der Milch, 43 (1894) p. 436.

Henkel. Ueber den Einfluss austrengender Bewegung auf die Milchproduction, 46 (1896) p. 329.

Kellner und Andrä. Versuche über den Einfluss der Verfütterung von Runkelrüben, getrockneten und gesäuerten Schnitzeln auf die Milchproduction, 49 (1898) p. 401.

Morgen. Versuche mit Milchkühen über den Einfluss der Arbeitsleistung auf die Menge und Zusammensetzung der produzierten Milch, 51 (1898) p. 117.

Landwirtschaftliche Jahrbücher.—Fleischmann. Untersuchung der Milch von sechszehn Kühen während der Dauer einer Lactation, 20 (1891) II, p. 1.

Kochs und Ramm. Verschiedenartig Zusammengesetzte Futterrationen in ihrer Wirkung auf die Milchsecretion und auf die Ausnutzung des Futters durch die Milchkühe, 21 (1892) p. 809.

Hittcher. Untersuchung der Milch von sechszehn Kühen des in Ostpreusnen rein gezüchteten holländischen Schlages während der Dauer einer Lactation, 23 (1894) p. 873.

Ramm. Versuche zur Ermittelung der Wirkung verschiedener Kraftfuttermittel auf die Milchergiebigkeit der Kühe. Ueber die Wirkung verschiedener Melassepräparate auf die Milchsecretion, 26 (1897) pp. 693, 732.

Maercker und Albert. Fütterungsversuche mit Milchkühen über den Einfluss fettreicher und fettarmer Kraftfuttermittel auf den Fettgehalt der Milch, 27 (1898) p. 188.

Hagemann. Beiträge zur rationellen Ernährung der Kühe, 24 (1895) p. 283 ; 26 (1897) p. 555 ; 28 (1899) p. 485.

Andrä. Die Waldplatterbse (Lathyrus silvestris), ihr Anbau und ihre Verwertung als Futter für Milchvieh, 31 (1902) p. 55.

Journal für Landwirtschaft.—Kühn. Versuche über den Einfluss der Ernährung auf die Milchproduction des Rindes, 25 (1877) p. 332.

Backhaus. Die Beeinflussung des Fettgehaltes der Milch durch verschiedene Kraftfuttermittel, 41 (1893) p. 328.

Milch Zeitung.—Klein. Futterungsversuch mit Sonnenblumen kuchen bei Milchkühen, 21 (1892) p. 673.

Kämmerer und Schlegel. Ueber den einfluss der Futternot auf dic Beschaffenheit der Milch, 24 (1895) p. 286.

Beglarian. Fütterungsversuche mit Leinöl und geschroteten Leinsamen an Milchkühe, 26 (1897) p. 522.

Rhodin. Futterung von Milchkühen mit Fett in Form von Emulsion, 27 (1898) pp. 306, 323.

Ramm und Winthrop. Versuche zur Ermittelung der Wirkung einiger neuer Futterstuffe auf die Milchsecretion unter Berücksichtigung des Fettgehaltes der mit Futtermitteln gebildeten Rationen, 27 (1898) p. 513.

Ramm und Müller. Fütterungsversuche an Milchkühe, 28 (1899), mit Tropon-Abfällen p. 17 ; mit Brauer-Schlempe p. 97 ; mit Illipenuss kuchen, p. 145 ; mit Palmkern-Illipekuchen, p. 225 ; mit Tropon, p. 241 ; mit Englisch Futterkuchen, p. 273.

Ramm. Fütterungsversuche an Milchkühe, 28 (1899) mit Maiskeim-melasse p. 641 ; mit Maiskleber, p. 658 ; mit Rohzucker, p. 673.

Momsen. Fütterungsversuche an Milchkühe mit Kürbissen, 29 (1900) p. 6.

Ramm, Momsen und Schumacker. Fütterungsversuche an Milchkühe mit Palmkernkuchen, 29 (1900) pp. 291, 309, 340, 353.

Vieth, Fütterungsversuche an Milchkühe mit Palmkernschrot 29 (1900) p. 294.

V. Resumés of Investigations of Effect of Food upon Milk.

Handbook of Experiment Station Work (Bulletin No. 15, Office of Experiment Stations) 1893, p. 209.

Milch Zeitung, 23 (1894), pp. 117–119, and 27 (1898), pp. 402–4.

Deut. Vierteljahr. off Gesund., 25, pp. 235–263.

Abs. in Molkerei Zeitung, 7 (1893), pp. 197–8.

Vermont Station Annual Report, 10 (1896–7), p. 152.

Experiment Station Record, 5 (1893–4), p. 967.

Agriculture of Maine, 1895.

Cornell University Agricultural Experiment Station, Bulletin No. 173, pp. 47–59.

Lightning Source UK Ltd.
Milton Keynes UK
UKHW012332061118
331891UK00010B/925/P